The Thr Dar...

Brother Hermenegild TOSF

Day of wrath and doom impending.
David's word with Sibyl's blending,
Heaven and earth in ashes ending.
Oh, what fear man's bosom rendeth,
When from heaven the Judge descendeth,
On whose sentence all dependeth.
Wondrous sound the trumpet flingeth;
Through earth's sepulchres it ringeth;
All before the throne it bringeth.
Death is struck, and nature quaking,
All creation is awaking,
To its Judge an answer making.
Lo, the book, exactly worded,
Wherein all hath been recorded,
Thence shall judgement be awarded.
When the Judge his seat attaineth,
And each hidden deed arraigneth,
Nothing unavenged remaineth.
What shall I, frail man, be pleading?
Who for me be interceding,
When the just are mercy needing?
King of Majesty tremendous,
Who dost free salvation send us,
Fount of pity, then befriend us!
Think, kind Jesu, my salvation
Caused Thy wondrous Incarnation;
Leave me not to reprobation.
Faint and weary, Thou hast sought me,
On the Cross of suffering bought me.
Shall such grace be vainly brought me?

Righteous Judge, for sin's pollution
Grant Thy gift of absolution,
Ere the day of retribution.
Guilty, now I pour my moaning,
All my shame with anguish owning;
Spare, O God, Thy suppliant groaning!
Through the sinful woman shriven,
Through the dying thief forgiven,
Thou to me a hope hast given.
Worthless are my prayers and sighing,
Yet, good Lord, in grace complying,
Rescue me from fires undying.
With Thy sheep a place provide me,
From the goats afar divide me,
To Thy right hand do Thou guide me.
When the wicked are confounded,
Doomed to flames of woe unbounded,
Call me with Thy saints surrounded.
Low I kneel, with heart's submission,
See, like ashes, my contrition,
Help me in my last condition.
Ah! that day of tears and mourning,
From the dust of earth returning
Man for judgement must prepare him,
Spare, O God, in mercy spare him.
Lord, all-pitying, Jesus blest,
Grant them Thine eternal rest. Amen.

Table of Contents

Introduction

We open with the Dies Irae, because it applies to the Three Days of Darkness. Pope Saint Gregory the Great says in his <u>Regula Pastoralis</u>: "Let them be told how the Prophet Sophonias holds out over them the stroke of divine reproof, when he says: 'Behold, the day of the Lord is coming, great and horrible . . . . That day is a day of wrath, a day of darkness and obscurity, a day of clouds and whirlwinds, a day of the trumpet and alarm against all the fenced cities and against all the high corners.'" [1] Note this verse inspired the Dies Irae.

The purpose of this book is to provide all of the prophecies that relate to the Three Days of Darkness. These are placed in a chronological order similar to that employed by Father Culleton is his two books, <u>Antichrist</u> and <u>The Prophets and Our Times</u>. They are provided without comment so that you can study the prophecies themselves. Some of the prophecies may appear out of place, but they will make sense as you move forward.

It is strongly recommended that you make notes as you proceed forward with this book. In this way you can sort things out for yourself.

Following the Three Days of Darkness prophecies are several other things. First a prophetic conjecture on what will happen and in what order followed by several other presentations, which the compiler considers may be useful.

---

[1] Sophonias 1:14-16. Gregory omits some expressions that would have made the warnings of the prophet still more terrible. The present passage, incidentally, gave Thomas of Celano the first line and keynote of his immortal sequence: *Dies irae, dies illa.*

The Three Days of Darkness In Prophecy

Sacred Scripture

Exodus 9:21-3: "And the Lord said to Moses: Stretch out they hand towards heaven: and may there be darkness upon the land of Egypt, so thick that it may be felt. And Moses stretch forth his hand towards heaven: and there came horrible darkness in all the land of Egypt for three days. No man saw his brother, nor moved himself out of the place where he was: but wheresoever the children of Israel dwelt there was light."

Isaias 1:28: "And he shall destroy the wicked, and the sinners together: and they that have forsaken the Lord, shall be consumed."

Isaias 4:1: "And in that day seven women shall take hold of one man, saying: We will eat our own bread, and wear our own apparel: only let us be called by thy name, take away our reproach."

Isaias 13:6-10: "Howl ye, for the day of the Lord is near: it shall come as a destruction from the Lord. Therefore shall all hands be faint, and every heart of man shall melt, And shall be broken. Gripings and pains shall take hold of them, they shall be in pain as a woman in labour. Every one shall be amazed at his neighbour, their countenances shall be as faces burnt. Behold, the day of the Lord shall come, a cruel day, and full of indignation, and of wrath, and fury, to lay the land desolate, and to destroy the sinners thereof out of it. For the stars of heaven, and their brightness shall not display their light: the sun shall be darkened in his rising, and the moon shall not shine with her light."

Ezechial 3:7-8: "And I will cover the Heavens then thou shalt be put out, and I will make the stars thereof dark. I will cover the sun with a cloud and the moon shall not giver her light. I will make all the lights of Heaven to mourn over thee: and I will cause darkness upon thy land, saith the Lord God, when thy wounded shall fall in the midst of the land, saith the Lord God."

Ezechial 22:29-31: "The people of the land have used oppression, and committed robbery: they afflicted the needy and poor, and they oppressed the stranger by calumny without judgment. And I sought among them for a man that might set up a hedge, and stand in the gap before me in favour of the land, that I might not destroy it: and I found none. And I poured out my indignation upon them, in the fire of my wrath I consumed them: I have rendered their way upon their own head, saith the Lord God."

Jeremias 30:7: "Alas, for that day is great, neither is there the like to it; and it is the time of tribulation to Jacob, but he shall be saved out of it."

Zacharias 13:7-9: "Awake, O sword, against my shepherd and against the man that cleaveth to me, saith the Lord of hosts. Strike the shepherd and the sheep shall be scattered. And I will turn my hand to the little ones. And they shall be in all the earth saith the Lord: two parts in it shall be scattered and perish, but the third part shall be left therein. And I will bring the third part through the fire and will refine them as silver is refined: and I will try them as gold is tried. They shall call on my name and I will hear them. I will say: Thou art my people. And they shall say: The Lord is my God."

Joel 1:15-16: "Ah, ah, ah, for the day: because the day of the Lord is at hand, and it shall come like destruction from the mighty. Is not your food cut off before your eyes, joy and gladness from the house of our God?"

Joel 2:1: "Blow ye the trumpet in Sion, sound an alarm in my holy mountain, let all the inhabitants of the land tremble: because the day of the Lord cometh, because it is nigh at hand,"

Joel 2:31: "The sun shall be turned into darkness and the moon into blood: before the great and dreadful day of the Lord doth come."

Joel 3:15: "The sun and moon are darkened: and the stars have withdrawn their shining."

Amos 5:18-20: " Woe to them that desire the day of the Lord: to what end is it for you? the day of the Lord is darkness, and not light. As if a man should flee from the face of a lion, and a bear should meet him: or enter into the house, and lean with his hand upon the wall, and a serpent should bite him. Shall not the day of the Lord be darkness, and not light: and obscurity, and no brightness in it?"

Amos 6:3-7: "You that are separated unto the evil day and that approach to the throne of iniquity; you that sleep upon beds of ivory and are wanton on your couches: that eat the lambs out of the flock and the calves out of the herd; you that sing to the sound of the psaltery: they have thought to have instruments of music like David; that drink wine in bowls and anoint themselves with the best annointments: and they are not concerned with the affliction of Joseph.

Wherefore now they shall go captive at the head of them that go into captivity: and the faction of the luxurious ones shall be taken away."

Amos 9:8-10: Behold the eyes of the Lord God are upon the sinful kingdom, and I will destroy it from the face of the earth: but yet I will not utterly destroy the house of Jacob, saith the Lord. For behold I will command, and I will sift the house of Israel among all nations, as corn is sifted in a sieve: and there shall not a little stone fall to the ground. All the sinners of my people shall fall by the sword: who say: The evils shall not approach, and shall not come upon us."

Jonas 2:1-11: "Now the Lord prepared a great fish to swallow up Jonas: and Jonas was in the belly of the fish three days and three nights. And Jonas prayed to the Lord his God out of the belly of the fish. And he said: I cried out of my affliction to the Lord, and he heard me: I cried out of the belly of hell, and thou hast heard my voice. And thou hast cast me forth into the deep in the heart of the sea, and a flood hath compassed me: all thy billows, and thy waves have passed over me. And I said: I am cast away out of the sight of thy eyes: but yet I shall see thy holy temple again. The waters compassed me about even to the soul: the deep hath closed me round about, the sea hath covered my head. I went down to the lowest parts of the mountains: the bars of the earth have shut me up for ever: and thou wilt bring up my life from corruption, O Lord my God. When my soul was in distress within me, I remembered the Lord: that my prayer may come to thee, unto thy holy temple. They that are vain observe vanities, forsake their own mercy. But I with the voice of praise will sacrifice to thee: I will pay whatsoever I have vowed for my salvation to the Lord. And the Lord spoke to the fish: and it vomited out Jonas upon the dry land."

Sophonias 1:3-10: "I will gather man and beast: I will gather the birds of the air and the fishes of the sea. And the ungodly shall meet with ruin: and I will destroy men from off the face of the land, saith the Lord. And I will stretch out my hand upon Juda and upon all the inhabitants of Jerusalem: and I will destroy out of this place the remnant of Baal and the names of the wardens of the temples with the priests. And them that worship the host of Heaven upon the tops of houses and them that adore and swear by the Lord and swear by Melchom. And them that turn away from following after the Lord and that have not sought the Lord nor searched after Him. Be silent before the face of the Lord God: for the day of the Lord is near, for the Lord hath prepared a victim, He hath sanctified His guests. And it shall come to pass in the day of the victim of the Lord that I will visit upon the king's sons and upon all such as are clothed in strange apparel. And I will visit in that day upon every one that entereth arrogantly over the threshold: them that fill the house of the Lord their God with iniquity and deceit. And there shall be in that day, saith the Lord, the noise of a cry from the fish gate and a howling from the Second and a great destruction from the hills."

Sophonias 2:10: "And this shall befall them for their pride: because they have blasphemed and have been magnified against the people of the Lord of hosts."

Micheas 3:11-12: "Her princes have judged for bribes, and her priests have taught for hire, and her prophets divined for money: and they leaned upon the Lord, saying: Is not the Lord in the midst of us? no evil shall come upon us. Therefore, because of you, Sion shall be ploughed as a field, and Jerusalem shall be as a heap of stones, and the mountain of the temple as the high places of the forests."

Matthew 24:29: "And immediately after the tribulation of those days, the sun shall be darkened and the moon shall not give her light, and the stars shall fall from heaven, and the powers of heaven shall be moved:"

Mark 13:23-25: "Take you heed therefore; behold I have foretold you all things. But in those days, after that tribulation, the sun shall be darkened, and the moon shall not give her light. And the stars of heaven shall be falling down, and the powers that are in heaven, shall be moved."

I Thessalonians 5:3: "For when they shall say peace and security; then shall sudden destruction come upon them, as the pains upon her that is with child, and they shall not escape."

Apocalypse 16:17-21: "And the seventh angel poured our his vial upon the air. And there came a great voice out of the temple from the throne, saying: It is done. And the were lightnings and voices and thunders: and there was a great earthquake, such an one as never had been seen since men were upon the earth, such an earthquake so great. And the great city was divided into three parts: and the cities of the Gentiles fell. And great Babylon came in remembrance before God, to give her the cup of the wine of the indignation of His wrath. And every island fled away: and the mountains were not found. And great hail, like a talent, came down from Heaven upon men: and men blasphemed God, for the plague of the hail: because it was exceedingly great."

Apocrypha

Enoch 91:7: "When sin and righteousness, blasphemy and violence and all kinds of deeds increase. and apostasy in transgression and uncleanness increase, a great chastisement shall come from Heaven."

IV Esdras 9:1-14: "He answered me then, and said, Measure thou the time diligently in itself: and when thou seest part of the signs past, which I have told thee before, then shalt thou understand, that it is the very same time, wherein the Highest will begin to visit the world which He made. Therefore when there shall be earthquakes and uproars of people in the world: Then shalt thou well understand, that the most High spake of those things from the days that were before thee, even from the beginning."

Apocalypse of Thomas: "On the fourth day at the first hour, the earth of the east shall speak, the abyss shall roar: then shall all the earth be moved by the strength of an earthquake. In that day shall all the idols of the heathen fall and all the buildings of the earth."

Private Prophecies

St. Hildegard (d. 1179)
"The time is coming when princes and people will renounce the authority of the Pope. Individual countries will prefer their own Church rulers to the Pope. The German Empire will be divided. Church property will be secularized. Priests will be persecuted. After the birth of Anti-Christ heretics will preach their false doctrines undisturbed. resulting in 'Christians having doubts about their holy Catholic faith:

"Toward the end of the world. mankind will be purified through sufferings. This will be true especially of the clergy. who will be robbed of all property. When the clergy has adopted a simple manner of living,. conditions will improve.

"A powerful wind will rise in the North carrying heavy fog and the densest dust by divine command and it will fill their throats and eyes so they will cease their savagery and be stricken with a great fear,

So after that there will be so few men left that seven women will fight for one man. that they will say to the man: 'marry me to take the disgrace from me': for in those days it will be a disgrace for a woman to be without child. as it was by the Jews in the Old Testament.

"Before the Comet comes, many nations, the good excepted, will be scoured with want and famine. The great nation in the ocean that is inhabited by people of different tribes and descent by an earthquake, storm and tidal waves will be devastated. It will be divided and in great part be submerged. That nation will also have many misfortunes at sea. and lose its colonies in the East through a Tiger and a Lion. The Comet by its tremendous pressure will force much out of the ocean and flood many countries. causing much want and many plagues. All sea coast cities will be fearful and many of them will be destroyed by tidal waves. and most living creatures will be killed and even those who escape will die from a horrible disease. For in none of those cities does a person live according to the laws of God.

"Peace will return to Europe when the white dower again takes possession of the throne of France. During this time of peace the people will be forbidden to carry weapons and iron will be used only for making agricultural implements and tools. Also during this period the soil will be very productive and many Jews, heathens and heretics will join the Church."

Sister Mary of Agreda (d. 1665)

"It was revealed to me that through the intercession of the Mother of God that all heresies will disappear. This victory over heresies has been reserved by Christ for His Blessed Mother. In the last times the Lord will especially spread the renown of His Mother: Mary began salvation and by her intercession it will be concluded. Before the second coming of Christ Mary must. more than ever, shine in mercy, might and grace in order to bring unbelievers into the Catholic Faith. The powers of Mary in the last times over the demons will be very conspicuous. Mary will extend the reign of Christ over the heathens and Mohammedans and it will be a time of great joy when Mary, as Mistress and Queen of Hearts, is enthroned. An unusual chastisement of the human race will take place towards the end of the world."

Blessed Casper del Bufalo (d. 1837)

He foretold "the destruction of impenitent persecutors of the Church during the three days darkness. He who outlives the darkness

11

and fear of the three days-it will seem to him as if he were alone on earth because of the fact that the world will be covered everywhere with carcasses."

Palma Maria d'Oria (d. 1863)

"There will be an attempt of the sectaries to establish a republican government in France. Spain. and Italy; a civil war will, in consequence, break out in those countries. Accompanied by other dreadful punishments. as pestilence and famine, the massacre of priests, and also of some dignitaries of the church. Rome shall have to endure severe trials from the malice of wicked men. But at the critical moment, when the rebellious Republicans shall attempt to take possession of the Holy City, they shall be suddenly arrested at the gates and forced to flyaway in terror. crushed under the deadly blows of the exterminating angel, who, in behalf of the Israelites. destroyed 185.000 men of Sennacherib's army.

"There shall be a three days darkness, during which the atmosphere will be infected by innumerable devils, who shall cause the death of large multitudes of incredulous and wicked men.

"Blessed candles alone shall be able to give light and preserve the faithful Catholics from this impending dreadful scourge. Supernatural prodigies shall appear in the heavens. There is to be a short but furious war, during which the enemies of religion and of mankind shall be universally destroyed. A general pacification of the world, and the universal triumph of the Church are to follow."

Sister Mary of Jesus Crucified of Pau (d. 1878)

"All states will be shaken by war and civil conflict. During a darkness lasting three days the people given to evil ways will perish so that only one-fourth of mankind will survive. The clergy, too, will be greatly reduced in number, as most of them will die in defense of the faith or of their country."

Marie Julie Jahenny of La Faudais (1891)

"There will come three days of continuous darkness. The blessed candle of wax alone will give light during the horrid darkness. One candle will last for three days, but in the houses of the Godless they will not give light. During those three days the demons will appear in abominable and horrible forms, they will make the air resound with shocking blasphemies. The lightning will penetrate the homes, but will not extinguish the light of the blessed candles; neither wind nor storm nor earthquake will extinguish it. Red clouds like blood will pass in the sky, the crash of thunder will make the earth tremble; lightning will flash through the streets at an unusual time of the year; the earth will tremble to its foundations; the ocean will cast its foaming waves over the land; the earth will be changed to an immense cemetery; the corpses of the wicked and the just will cover the face of the earth. The famine that follows will be great. All vegetation will be destroyed as well as three-fourths of the human race. The crisis will come all of a sudden and chastisement will be world wide."

Blessed Anna Maria Taigi (d. 1837)

"God will ordain two punishments: One, in the form of wars, revolutions and other evils. will originate on earth: the other will be sent from Heaven. There shall come over all the earth an intense darkness lasting three days and three nights. Nothing will be visible and the air will be laden with pestilence, which will claim principally but not exclusively the enemies of religion. During this darkness artificial light will be impossible. Only blessed candles can be lighted and will afford illumination. He who out of curiosity opens his window to look out or leaves his house will fall dead on the spot. During these three days the people should remain in their homes, pray the Rosary and beg God for mercy.

"On this terrible occasion so many of these wicked men, enemies of His Church, and of their God, shall be killed by this divine scourge, that their corpses round Rome will be as numerous as the fish, which a recent inundation of the Tiber had carried into the city. All the enemies of the Church. Secret as well as known, will perish over the whole earth during that universal darkness, with the exception of some few, whom God will soon after convert. The air shall be infected by demons, who will appear under all sorts of hideous forms.

"After the three days of darkness, Saints Peter and Paul, having come down from heaven. will preach throughout the world and designate a new pope. A great light will flash from their bodies and will settle upon the cardinal, the future Pontiff. Then Christianity will spread throughout the world. Whole nations will join the Church shortly before the reign of Anti-Christ. These conversions will be amazing. Those who shall survive shall have to conduct themselves well. There shall be innumerable conversions of heretics. who will return to the bosom of the Church; all will note the edifying conduct of their lives. as well as that of all other Catholics. Russia, England. and China will come into the Church.

"France shall fall into frightful anarchy. The French people shall have a desperate civil war, in which old men themselves will take up arms. The political parties having exhausted their blood and their rage. without being able to arrive at any satisfactory understanding, shall at the last extremity agree by common consent to have recourse to the Holy See. Then the Pope shall send to France a special legate, in order that he may examine the state of affairs and the dispositions of the people. In consequence of the information received. His Holiness himself shall nominate a most Christian king for the government of France."

"Religious shall be persecuted. priests shall be massacred. the churches shalt be closed. but only for a short time; the Holy Father shall be obliged to abandon Rome."

The Blessed Virgin Mary to Teresa Musco, August 31, 1951: "God will send a great chastisement to all the human race in the second half of the 20th century, when Satan arrives at the summit of the Church ... In 1972 will begin the time of Satan."

Julia of Yugoslavia, a seeress known to Cardinal Stepinach and Pope Pius XII

"The people will realize in the end who it is they have disobeyed. Retain My instructions for the days when there is only a small flock left; they will hunger and hear My words. I led you to My Vicar...in the days after the terrible affliction I shall renew My earth."

"The meaning of the darkness you saw is that man's sins are too dark and that it has poisoned everything on the earth and the atmosphere and the teachings of my servants....

"The sun that gives heat to the earth is my symbol, its creator. Because they do not see me anywhere, the faithless deny my existence and me. Whoever lives after the big disaster will be able to see me directly. I will hover above the small group of sheep of that day.

"In those days, there will be only one shepherd and one faith, that is, the Catholic Church I established when I was on the earth. After the disaster that I cause to fall on my hard-hearted people on the earth, a good and sanctified generation will be formed and the earth will be made abundant with my blessing. My sons and daughters will follow my commandments."

14

Padre Pio

It should be noted that in several warnings from the Holy Office, it is forbidden to write books about Padre Pio of Pietrelcina. However, his own writings are not forbidden by the Holy Office. [2]

What follows below is compiled from two resources. The first was circulated widely in the very early 1970's. The balance appears on the internet. These do overlap, but give a good summary of the Three Days of Darkness.

THE THREE DAYS DARKNESS
Predictions by Padre Pio

These are the words of Our Lord spoken to a Capuchin priest, Father Pio, who has borne the stigmata for over fifty years.

How unconcerned men are concerning these things which shall come upon them, contrary to all expectations. How indifferent they are in preparing themselves for these unheard of events through which they will soon have to pass. Prayers, prayers and again prayers I desire of you. When the Angel of Death with the avenging sword of justice shall begin to mow down, and Hell in uproar and rage shall cast itself upon the just to destroy you with their frightening terrors, then it is your faith and confidence in Me must be firm as a rock. I will protect you. I will give you a warning which will indicate the beginning of My threatening judgment.

One cold winter night this catastrophe shall come upon the earth like a flash of lightning -- at which moment the light of the morning sun shall be replaced by black darkness. No one shall leave the house or look out of a window. From that moment I Myself shall appear midst thunder and lightning...The wicked shall behold My Divine Heart. There shall be great confusion because of this utter darkness in which the entire world shall be enveloped and many, many shall die from fear and despair. Those who shall fight for My cause shall receive grace from My Divine Heart. The cry, "Who is like unto God" shall serve as a

---

[2] AAS 150356, May 31, 1923; AAS 16-368, July 24, 1924; AAS 18-186, April 23, 1926; AAS 23-233; May 22, 1931. These have never been removed by the One Holy Catholic Church.

means of protection to many. Many, however, shall burn in the open fields like grass. The godless shall be annihilated so that afterwards the just shall be able to start afresh. On that day, as soon as complete darkness has set in, no one shall leave the house or look out the window. Talk to no one outside the house. Those who disregard this advice will be killed instantly. The darkness shall last a day and a night, followed by another day and night and yet another day, but on the following night the stars shall shine again, and on the next morning the sun shall rise again.

Then shall My elect not sleep as did the disciples in the Garden of Olives. They shall pray incessantly, and they shall not be disappointed in Me. I shall gather My elect...Hell will believe itself in possession of the entire earth, but I shall reclaim it. Do you perhaps think that I would permit My Father to have such terrible chastisement come upon the world if it would turn from iniquity to justice? But because of My love, these, afflictions shall be permitted to come upon men, and although many shall curse, yet thousands of souls shall be saved through them. No human understanding can fathom the depth of My love. Pray, pray, I desire prayers.

My love for men is very great, especially for those who give themselves entirely to Me. Pray and make reparation to Me. Admonish others to do the same, because they have not heeded My graces. Persevere so that your adversary shall have no dominion over you. Tell them to be prepared at all times, for My judgment shall come upon them suddenly, and when least expected, and no one shall escape My hands. I shall find them all. I shall protect the just. Watch the sun and the stars of the heavens; when they appear to be unduly disturbed and restless, know that the day is not far off. Stay united in prayer and watching until the Angel of destruction has passed your doors. Pray that these days will be shortened. Wickedness has reached its climax and the punishment can no longer be delayed. Tell all men that the time has come in which these things shall be fulfilled.

Pray, make reparation, be fervent, practice mortification. Great things are at stake...I or your adversary, the devil. The measure of sin is filled...The day of revenge with its terrifying happenings is near, nearer that you imagine. As the world is sleeping in false security, the Divine judgment shall strike them like a thunderbolt. The godless and wicked people shall be destroyed without mercy. Keep your windows covered.

Do not look out. Light a blessed candle, one of which will suffice for the day. Pray the rosary, read spiritual books and make acts of spiritual communion. Also acts of love which are so pleasing to Me. Pray with outstretched arms or prostrate on the floor, in order that many souls will be saved. Do not go outside the house. Provide yourself with sufficient food. The powers of nature shall be moved and a rain of fire shall make people tremble for fear. Have courage, I am In the midst of you. Take care of the animals during these days. I shall give you a few signs beforehand at which time place some food before them. I will preserve the property of the elect, which includes the animals. For the just shall be in need of sustenance afterwards as well. Let no one go across the yard to feed the animals. He who steps outside shall perish. Cover your windows carefully. My elect shall not see My wrath. Have confidence in Me...I will protect you. Your confidence honors Me and obliges Me to come to your aid. My dear Mother Mary, St. Elizabeth, St. Conrad, St. Peter, the Little Flower, St. Therese, and your Holy angels shall be your intercessors...implore their aid. Be courageous soldiers of Christ.

Over 70 seers of great sanctity and veracity have foretold this Divine punishment, which is often called the three days darkness. According to their predictions, this punishment will come suddenly, be universal and wipe out three quarters of mankind. During it electric lights will not burn, hence the faithful should light a blessed candle and pray the ROSARY for protection. [3]

January 28, 1950

Keep your windows well covered. Do not look out. Light a blessed candle, which will suffice for many days. Pray the rosary. Read spiritual books. Make acts of Spiritual Communion, also acts of love, which are so pleasing to Us. Pray with outstretched arms, or prostrate on the ground, in order that many souls may be saved. Do not go outside the house. Provide yourself with sufficient food. The powers of nature shall be moved and a rain of fire shall make people tremble with fear. Have courage! I am in the midst of you.

February 7, 1950

---

[3] This appears on the original circulated in 1970 and is included here.

Take care of the animals during these days. I am the Creator and Preserver of all animals as well as man. I shall give you a few signs beforehand, at which time you should place more food before them. I will preserve the property of the elect, including the animals, for they shall be in need of sustenance afterwards as well. Let no one go across the yard, even to feed the animals--he who steps outside will perish! Cover your windows carefully. My elect shall not see My wrath. Have confidence in Me, and I will be your protection. Your confidence obliges Me to come to your aid.

The hour of My coming is near! But I will show mercy. A most dreadful punishment will bear witness to the times. My angels, who are to be the executioners of this work, are ready with their pointed swords! They will take special care to annihilate all those who mocked Me and would not believe in My revelations.

Hurricanes of fire will pour forth from the clouds and spread over the entire earth! Storms, bad weather, thunderbolts and earthquakes will cover the earth for two days. An uninterrupted rain of fire will take place! It will begin during a very cold night. All this is to prove that God is the Master of Creation. Those who hope in Me, and believe in my words, have nothing to fear because I will not forsake them, nor those who spread My message. No harm will come to those who are in the state of grace and who seek My mother's protection.

That you may be prepared for these visitations, I will give you the following signs and instructions: The night will be very cold. The wind will roar. After a time, thunderbolts will be heard. Lock all the doors and windows. Talk to no one outside the house. Kneel down before a crucifix, be sorry for your sins, and beg My Mother's protection. Do not look during the earthquake, because the anger of God is holy! Jesus does not want us to behold the anger of God, because God's anger must be contemplated with fear and trembling.

Those who disregard this advice will be killed instantly. The wind will carry with it poisonous gases which will be diffused over the entire earth. Those who suffer and die innocently will be martyrs and they will be with Me in My Kingdom.

Satan will triumph! But after three nights, the earthquake and fire will cease. On the following day the sun will shine again. angels will descend from Heaven and will spread the spirit of peace over the earth.

A feeling of immeasurable gratitude will take possession of those who survive this terrible ordeal-the impending punishment-with which God has visited the earth since creation.

I have chosen souls in other countries too, such as Belgium, Switzerland. Spain, who have received these revelations so that other countries also may be prepared. Pray much during this Holy Year of 1950. Pray the Rosary, but pray it well, so that your prayers may reach Heaven. Soon a more terrible catastrophe shall come upon the entire world, such as never before has been witnessed, a terrible chastisement never before experienced! The war of 1950 shall be the introduction to these things.

How unconcerned men are regarding these things! which shall so soon come upon them, contrary to all expectations. How indifferent they are in preparing themselves for these unheard of events, through which they will have to pass so shortly!

The weight of the Divine balance has reached the earth! The wrath of My Father shall be poured out over the entire world! I am again warning the world through your instrumentality, as I have so often done heretofore.

The sins of men have multiplied beyond measure: Irreverence in Church, sinful pride committed in sham religious activities, lack of true brotherly love, indecency in dress, especially at summer seasons...The world is filled with iniquity.

This catastrophe shall come upon the earth like a flash of lightning at which moment the light of the morning sun shall be replaced by black darkness! No one shall leave the house or look out of a window from that moment on. I Myself shall come amidst thunder and lightning. The wicked shall behold My Divine Heart. There shall be great confusion because of this utter darkness in which the entire earth shall be enveloped, and many, many shall die from fear and despair.

Those who shall fight for My cause shall receive grace from My Divine Heart; and the cry: "WHO IS LIKE UNTO GOD!" shall serve as a means of protection to many. However, many shall burn in the open fields like withered grass! The godless shall be annihilated, so that afterwards the just shall be able to stand afresh.

On the day, as soon as complete darkness has set in, no one shall leave the house or look from out of the window. The darkness shall last a day and a night, followed by another day and a night, and another day--but on the night following, the stars will shine again, and on the next morning the sun shall rise again, and it will be SPRINGTIME!!

In the days of darkness, My elect shall not sleep, as did the disciples in the garden of olives. They, shall pray incessantly, and they shall not be disappointed in Me. I shall gather My elect. Hell will believe itself to be in possession of the entire earth, but I shall reclaim it!

Do you, perhaps, think that I would permit My Father to have such terrible chastisements come upon the world, if the world would turn from iniquity to justice? But because of My great love, these afflictions shall be permitted to come upon man. Although many shall curse Me, yet thousands of souls shall be saved through them. No human understanding can fathom the depth of My love!

Pray! Pray! I desire your prayers. My Dear Mother Mary, Saint Joseph, Saint Elizabeth, Saint Conrad, Saint Michael. Saint Peter, the Little Therese, Your Holy Angels, shall be your intercessors. Implore their aid! Be courageous soldiers of Christ! At the return of light, let everyone give thanks to the Holy Trinity for Their protection! The devastation shall be very great! But I, Your God, will have purified the earth. I am with you. Have confidence! (Here ends Padre Pio's Message)

Prophetic Overview

Events happen in a certain order. This author believes that the following order makes sense.

First of all we have four events occur in a rather rapid succession. The first is the coming of Antichrist. Antichrist then usurps the Papacy. Following this he replaces the Holy Sacrifice of the Mass with the abomination of desolation. This is the beginning of the time called the Great Apostasy based upon II Thessalonians chapter 2.

After the death of Antichrist the destruction continues until God finally intervenes with the Three Days of Darkness. This is followed by the Universal Conversion when there truly will be one flock and one shepherd. Saint John Eudes says: "All the holy Fathers [4] agree that after the death of antichrist the whole world will be converted." We should remember that when the Fathers of the Church are in total agreement on a matter, the Church considers their opinion to be infallibly true.

But first let us consider Henry Edward Cardinal Manning's opinion on what must some day happen to the Catholic Church. Indeed he is of the opinion that the Church will be reduced to a handful, which is borne out by the prophet Isaias, when he says: "And they that remain of the trees of his forest shall be so few, that they shall easily be numbered, and a child shall write them down." [5]

---

[4] Dionysius the Carthusian in cap. 3, Epist. 1, ad Thess; Cornelius a Lapide in cap. 2, Epist. Ad Rom. Verse 15.
[5] Isaias 10:19

Cardinal Manning on the Great Apostasy

Before we enter upon the last subject which remains, let us take up the point at which we broke off in the last Lecture. It was this, that there are upon earth two great antagonists—on the one side, the spirit and the principle of evil; and on the other, the incarnate God manifested in His Church, but eminently in His Vicar, who is His representative, the depository of His prerogatives and therefore His special personal witness, speaking and ruling in His name. The office of the Vicar of Jesus Christ contains, in fullness, the Divine prerogatives of the Church: forasmuch as, being the special representative of the Divine Head, he bears all His communicable powers in the government of the Church on earth solely and alone. The other bishops and pastors, who are united with him, and act in subordination to him, cannot act without him; but he may act alone, possessing a plenitude of power in himself. And further, the endowments of the body are the prerogatives of the head and, therefore, the endowments which descend from the Divine Head of the Church upon the whole mystical body are centred in the head of that body upon earth; forasmuch as he stands in the place of the Incarnate Word as the minister and witness of the Kingdom of God among men. Now, it is against that person eminently and emphatically, as said before, that the spirit of evil and of falsehood direct its assault; for if the head of the body be smitten, the body itself must die. "Smite the shepherd, and the sheep shall be scattered," was the old guile of the evil one, who smote the Son of God that he might scatter the flock. But that craft has been once tried, and foiled for ever; for in the death which smote the Shepherd, the flock was redeemed: and through the shepherd who is constituted in the place of the Son be smitten, the flock can be scattered no more. Three hundred years the world strove to cut off the line of the Sovereign Pontiffs; but the flock was never scattered: and so it shall be to the end. It is, nevertheless, against the Church of God, and above all against its Head, that all the spirits of evil in all ages, and, above all, in the present, direct the shafts of their enmity. We see, therefore, what it is that hinders the manifestation, the supremacy, and the dominion of the spirit of evil and of disorder upon earth—namely, the constituted order of Christendom, the supernatural society of which the Catholic Church has been the creator, the bond of union, and the principle of conservation; and the head of that Church, who is eminently the principle of order—the centre of the Christian society which binds the nations of the world in peace. Now the subject which remains to us is far more difficult. It reaches into the future, and deals with agencies so transcendent and mysterious, that all I shall venture to do will be to sketch in outline what the broad and luminous prophecies, especially of the book of Daniel and of the Apocalypse, set forth; without attempting to enter into minute details, which can only be interpreted by the event.

And further, as I said in the beginning, I shall not attempt anything except under the direct guidance of the theology of the Church, and of writers whose works have its approbation. As I have ventured hitherto nothing of my own, so until the end I shall pursue the same course.

What I have, then, to speak of is, the persecution of Antichrist, and finally his destruction.

First of all, let us begin with the twenty-fourth chapter of the holy Gospel according to St. Matthew, in which we read that our Divine Lord said when He beheld the buildings of the Temple, "There shall not be left here a stone upon a stone that shall not be destroyed." And His disciples, when He was in the Mount of Olives, Came to Him privately and said, Tell us what will be the sign of Thy coming, and of the consummation of the world." They understood that the destruction of the Temple in Jerusalem and the end of the world should be part of one and the same action, and should take place at one and the same time. Now, as in nature we see mountains foreshortened one against another, so that the whole chain shares but one form, so in the events of prophecy, there are here two different events which appear but one the destruction of Jerusalem, and the end of the world. Our Divine Lord went on to tell them that there should come such a tribulation as had never yet been; and that unless those days were shortened, there should no flesh be saved; that for the sake of the elect those days should be shortened; that kingdom should rise against kingdom, and nation against nation, and there should be wars and pestilences and famines in divers places; that brethren should betray their brethren to death, (Mark 13) that they should be persecuted for His Name's sake, that all men should hate them, that they should be put to death, and that false Christs and false prophets should arise and should seduce many; that is, there should come false teachers, pretended Messias; and that in the midst of all these persecutions Himself would come to judgment—that, like as the lightning cometh out of the east, and appeareth even unto the west, so shall also the coming of the Son of Man be.

In this answer our Divine Lord spoke of two events—one, the destruction of Jerusalem, and the other, the end of the world. The one has been fulfilled, and the other is yet, to come. This chapter of St. Matthew will afford us a key to the interpretation of' the Apocalypse. That book may be divided into four parts. The first part describes the Church on earth, under the seven Churches to which the messages were sent by our Divine Lord. They represent, as a constellation, the whole Church on earth. The second part relates to the destruction of Judaism, and the overthrow of the Jewish people. The third part relates to the persecution of the church by the pagan city of Rome, and to its overthrow: and the fourth and last part relates to the peace of the Church under the figure of the heavenly Jerusalem corning down from heaven and dwelling among men. Many interpreters, especially the early age, and also writers such as Bossuet and others of a later date, have supposed the prophecies of the Apocalypse, excepting only the last chapters, to be fulfilled by the events which took place in the first six centuries—that the overthrow of Jerusalem, the persecution of the Church, and the destruction of pagan Rome. But it is the nature of prophecy gradually to unfold itself. As I said of mountains foreshortened to our sight, when we wind about their base, they begin, as it were, to disentangle their outlines and to reveal themselves as many and distinct; so it is with the events of prophecy. The action of the world moves in cycles; that is, as the wise man says, "what hath been shall be," and "there is nothing new under the sun;" and that which we have seen in the beginning, prophecy declares shall be once more at the end of the world. In the four divisions of the Book Apocalypse, we have seen chief agents: the Church, the Jews, and persecuting power, which was pagan Rome. Now, these three at this moment exist upon earth. There is the Church of God still; there is the ancient people of God, the Jewish race, still preserved, as we have already seen, by a mysterious providence, for some future instrumentality; and there is, thirdly, the natural society of man without God, which took the form of paganism of old, and will take the form of infidelity in the last days. These three are the ultimate agents in the history of the modern world: first, the natural society of mankind; next, the dispersion of the Jewish people; and, thirdly, the universal Church The two last are the only bodies which interpenetrate into all nations and have an unity distinct and independent of them. They have greater power than any nation, and are deadly and changeless antagonists. Now the Church has had to undergo already two persecutions, one from the hand of the Jews and one also from the hand of the pagans; so the writers of the early ages, the Fathers both of the East and of the West, foretold that, in the last age of the world, the Church will have to undergo a third persecution, more bitter, more bloody, more searching, and more fiery than any it has undergone as yet, and that from the hands of an infidel world revolted from the Incarnate Word. And therefore the Book Apocalypse, like the prophecy of St. Matthew, reveals two events, or two actions. There is the event which is past, the type and the shadow of the event to come, and there is the event which is still future, at the end of the world; and all the persecutions that have ever been hitherto are no more than the forerunners and the types of the last persecution which shall be.

We have already seen the parallel of the two mysteries, the mystery of impiety and the mystery of godliness; and also the parallel of the two cities, the City of God and the city of this world. There remains another parallel which it is necessary that we should examine in order to make clear that which I shall have to say hereafter. We read in the Book Apocalypse of two women. There is a woman clothed with the sun, and there is a woman sitting upon a beast covered with the names of blasphemy. Now it is clear that these two women, like the two mysteries and the two cities, represent again two antagonist spirits, two antagonist principles. In the twelfth chapter of the Book Apocalypse we read of the woman "clothed with the sun," having "the moon under her feet, and on her head a crown of twelve stars." No Catholic will be at a loss for an interpretation of these words; and even Protestant interpreters, in order to avoid seeing the immaculate Mother of God in this woman clothed with the sun, tell us that it signifies the Church. In this they are perfectly right,—only they speak but half the truth. The woman typifies or symbolises the Church, for this reason, that the symbol of the Church is the Incarnation, the woman with the child; the symbol of the Incarnation is the Mother of

God. On the other hand, we need not go far to find the interpretation of the woman who sits upon the beast having the names of blasphemy, for the last verse of the seventeenth chapter says "The woman which thou sawest is the great city which hath kingdom over the kings of the earth." It is quite clear, then, the there is an antagonism between these two women —the Church under the symbol of the Incarnation, and the great city, the city of Rome, with the seven hills, which has kingdom over the kings the earth.

Now let us keep clearly in mind this distinction because interpreters, heated by the spirit of controversy, have been pleased to confound these two things together, and to tell us that this woman seated on the beast is the Church of Rome. But the Church of Rome is the Church of God, or least a part of it, even in the mind of these interpreters. How, then, can these two, which so contrary the one to the other, mean the same thing? In truth, as it was with Elymas magician, who, for his perverseness, could not hold the sun for a season, so they who heat themselves in controversy lose their sense. In the splendor of this vision they cannot see the truth, and about to find the Church of God in that which the type of its antagonist; fulfilling again the end self-deceit, that when the truth is upon earth mistake a falsehood for the truth, as when the true Christ was come, they knew Him not, and called Him Antichrist. As it was with His Person, so it is with His Church.

With these preliminary distinctions, let us begin the last part of our subject. What I have to speak of is the persecution which Antichrist shall inflict upon the Church of God. We have already seen reason to believe that as our Divine Lord delivered Himself into the hands of sinners when His time was come, and no man could lay hand upon Him, until of His own free will He delivered Himself over to their power, so in like manner it shall be with that Church of which He said, "Upon this rock will I build my Church, and the gates of hell shall not prevail against it." As the wicked did not prevail against Him even when they bound Him with cords, dragged Him to the judgment, blindfolded His eyes, mocked Him as a false King, smote Him on the head as a false Prophet, led Him away, crucified Him, and in the mastery of their power seemed to have absolute dominion over Him, so that He lay ground down and almost annihilated under their feet; and as, at that very time when He was dead and buried out of their sight, He was conqueror over all, and rose again the third day, and ascended into heaven, and was crowned, glorified, and invested with His royalty, and reigns supreme, King of kings and Lord of lords,—even shall it be with His Church: though for a time persecuted, and, to the eyes of man, overthrown and trampled on, dethroned, despoiled, mocked, and crushed, yet in that high time of triumph the gate of hell shall not prevail. There is in store for the Church of God a resurrection and an ascension, a royalty and a dominion, a recompense of glory for all it has endured. Like Jesus, it needs must suffer on the way to its crown; yet crowned it shall be with Him eternally. Let no one, then, be scandalised if the prophecy speak of sufferings to come. We are fond of imagining triumphs and glories for the Church on earth,—that the Gospel is to be preached to all nations, and the world to be converted, and all enemies subdued, and I know not what,—until some ears are impatient of hearing that there is in store for the Church a time of terrible trial: and so we do as the Jews of old, who looked for a conqueror, a king, and for prosperity; and when their Messias came in humility and in passion, they did not know Him. So, I am afraid, many among us intoxicate their minds with the visions of success and victory, and cannot endure the thought that there is a time of persecution yet to come for the Church of God. Let us hear, therefore, the words of the prophet Daniel. Speaking of the person whom St. John calls the Antichrist, whom he calls the king that shall work according to his own will, the prophet Daniel says, "He shall speak words against the High One,"—that is, the Almighty God,—"and shall crush the saints of the Most High." Again he says, "It"—that is, the power of this king—"was magnified even unto the strength of heaven: and it threw down of the strength, and of the stars and trod upon them. And it was magnified even to the prince of the strength: and it took away from him the continual sacrifice, and cast down the place of his sanctuary." Further, he says, "The victim and the sacrifice shall fail, and there shall be in the temple the abomination of desolation." These three passages are taken from the seventh, and the eighth, and the ninth chapters of Daniel. I might add more, but they are enough, for in the Book Apocalypse (12:7) we find a key to these words. St. John, evidently referring to the Book of Daniel, writes of the beast, that is, the persecuting power which shall reign on the earth by might, "It was given unto him to make war with the saints and to overcome them." Now here we have four distinct prophecies of a persecution which shall be inflicted by this antichristian power upon the Church of God. I will therefore point out as briefly as I can what appears in the events now around us to be leading on to this result.

1. The first sign or mark of this coming persecution is an indifference to truth. Just as there is dead calm before a whirlwind, and as the waters over a great fall run like glass, so before an outbreak there is a time of tranquillity. The first sign is indifference. The sign that portends more surely than any other the outbreak of a future persecution is a sort of scornful indifference to truth or falsehood. Ancient Rome in its might and power adopted every false religion from all its conquered nations, and gave to each of them a temple within its walls. It was sovereignly and contemptuously indifferent to all the superstitions of the earth. It encouraged them; for each nation had its own proper superstition, and that proper superstition was a mode of tranquillising, of governing, and of maintaining in subjection, the people who were indulged by building a temple within its gates. In like manner we see the nations of the Christian world at this moment gradually adopting every form of religious contradiction—that is, giving it full scope, and, as it is called, perfect toleration; not recognising any distinctions of truth or falsehood between one religion or another, but leaving all forms of religion to work their own way. I am not saying a word against this system if it be inevitable. It is the only system whereby freedom of conscience is now maintained. I only say, miserable is the state of the world in which ten thousand poisons grow round one truth; miserable is the state of any country where truth is only tolerated. This is a state of great spiritual and intellectual danger; and yet it seems there is no alternative but that the civil governors leave perfect freedom of conscience, and therefore maintain themselves in a state of perfect indifference.

Let us see the result. First of all, the divine voice of the Church of God is thereby entirely ignored. They see no distinction between a doctrine of faith and a human opinion. Both are allowed to have free way. There are mixed together doctrines of faith with every form of heresy, until, as in England, we have all conceivable forms of belief, from the Council of Trent in all its rigour and in all its perfection, on the one hand, to the *Catechism of Positive Religion* on the other. We have every form of opinion started, and freely allowed, from the two extremes; the one of which is the worship of God in Unity and Trinity, incarnate for us; and the other, the denial of God, and the worship of humanity. Next, denying and ignoring of course the divine voice of the Church, the civil governor must ignore the divine unity of the Church, and admit every form of separation, or system, or division all mingled together; so that the people are crumbled into religious sects and religious divisions, and the law of unity is entirely lost. Then, again, all positive truth, as such, is despised; and it is despised, because who shall say who is right and who is wrong, if there be no Divine teacher? If there be no Divine judge, who shall say what is true and what is false between conflicting religious opinions? A state that has separated itself from the unity of the Church, and thereby has lost the guidance of the Divine teacher, is unable to determine by any of its tribunals, civil or ecclesiastical. as it may continue to call them, what is true and what is false in a controverted question of religion; and then, as we know, there grows up an intense hatred of what is called dogmatism, that is, of any positive truth, any thing definite, any thing final, anything which has precise limits, any form of belief which is expressed in particular definitions—all this is utterly distasteful to men who on principle encourage all forms of religious opinion. In fact, we are coming to the state of Festus, who, when he heard that the Jews had an accusation against St. Paul, reported that he could find "no question which seemed ill" to him, because they were questions superstition, and "about one Jesus deceased, whom Paul affirmed to be alive." [6] Now this is just the state of indifference to which the civil governors of the world are gradually reducing themselves, and the government they administer, and the people they govern.

2. The next step is, then, the persecution of the truth. When Rome in ancient days legalised every idolatry throughout the whole of the Roman Empire, there was one religion which was called a religio illicita, an unlawful religion, and there was one society which was called a societas illicita, or an unlawful society. They might worship the twelve gods of Egypt, or Jupiter Capitolinus, or Dea Roma; but they might not worship the God of heaven, they might not worship God, revealed in His Son. They did not believe in the Incarnation; and that one religion which was alone true was the only religion that was not tolerated. There were the priests of Jupiter, of Cybele, of Fortune, and of Vesta; there were all manner of sacred confraternities, and orders,

---

[6] Acts 20:18-19

and societies, and I know not what; but there was one society which was not permitted to exist, and that was the Church of the living God. In the midst of this universal toleration, there was one exception made with the most peremptory exactness, to exclude the truth and the Church of God from the world. Now this is what must again inevitably come to pass, because the Church of God is inflexible in the mission committed to it. The Catholic Church will never compromise a doctrine; it will never allow two doctrines to be taught within its pale; it will never obey the civil governor pronouncing judgment in matters that are spiritual. The Catholic Church is bound by the Divine law to suffer martyrdom rather than compromise a doctrine, or obey the law of the civil governor which violates the conscience; and more than this, it is not only bound to offer a passive disobedience, which may be done in a corner, and therefore not detected, and because not detected not punished; but the Catholic Church cannot be silent; it cannot hold its peace; it cannot cease to preach the doctrines of Revelation, not only of the Trinity and of the Incarnation, but likewise of the Seven Sacraments, and of the infallibility of the Church of God, and of the necessity of unity, and of the sovereignty, both spiritual and temporal, of the Holy See; and because it will not be silent, and cannot compromise, and will not obey in matters that are of its own Divine prerogative, therefore it stands alone in the world; for there is not another Church so called, nor any community professing to be a Church, which does not submit, or obey, or hold its peace, when the civil governors of the world command. It is not ten years since we heard of a decision on the matter of baptism, involving the doctrine of original sin on the one hand, and the doctrine of preventing grace on the other; and because a civil judge pronounced that it was lawful in the Established Church of England for men without punishment to teach two contradictory doctrines, bishops, priests, and people were content that it should be so: or, at least, they said, "We cannot do otherwise; the civil power will allow men to preach both: what can we do? We are persecuted, and therefore we hold our peace; we go on ministering under a civil law which compels us to endure that the man who preaches before us in the morning, or the man who shall preach after us in the afternoon, may preach a doctrine in diametrical contradiction to that which we know to be the revealed doctrine of God; and because the civil governors have determined it so, we are not responsible, and the Established Church is not responsible, because it is persecuted." Now this is the characteristic difference between a human system established by the civil law and the Church of God. Would it be permitted in the Church which is Catholic and Roman, that I should now deny that every child baptised receives the infusion of regenerating grace? What would become of me by tomorrow morning? You know perfectly well that if I were to depart one jot or one tittle from the Holy Catholic faith, delivered by the Divine voice of the Church of God, I should be immediately suspended. and no civil governor, or power in the world, could restore me to the exercise of my faculties; no civil judge or potentate on earth could restore me to the administration of the Sacraments, until the spiritual authority of the Church permitted me to do so.

This, then, is the characteristic difference, which must one day bring down upon the Church, in all countries where this spirit of indifference has established itself, a persecution of the civil power. And for a further reason, because the difference between the Catholic Church and every other society is this other societies are of voluntary formation; that is, people unite themselves to a particular body, and, they do not like it on better knowledge, they go their way: they become Baptists, or Anabaptists, or Episcopalians, or Unitarians, or Presbyterians, until they find something which they do not like in these stems; and then they go their way, and either unite themselves to some other body or remain unattached; because the societies have no claim to govern the will,—all that they profess to do is to teach. They are like the ancient school, and their teaching is a kind of Christian philosophy. They put their doctrines before those who are willing to listen, and if they listen, and, by good fortune agree with them, they remain with them: if not. they go their way. But where is the government over the will? Can they say, "In the name of God, and under pain of mortal sin, you must believe that God was incarnate, and that our incarnate Lord offers Himself in sacrifice upon the altar, that the Sacraments instituted by the Son of God are seven, and that they all convey the grace of the Holy Ghost" Unless they have an authority over the will as well as over the intelligence, they are only a school, and not a kingdom. Now this is a character entirely wanting in every society that cannot claim to govern in the name of our Divine Lord, and with a Divine voice and therefore the Church of God differs from every other society in this particular, that it is not only a communion of people who voluntarily unite together, but that it is a kingdom, It has a legislature; the line of its councils for eighteen hundred years have deliberated, and decreed with all the solemnity and the majesty of an imperial parliament. It has executive which carries out and enforces the decree of those councils with all the calmness and all the peremptory decision of an imperial will. The Church of God, therefore, is an empire within an empire; and the governors and princes of this world are jealous of it for that very reason. They say, "Nolumus hunc regnare super nos"—"we will not have this man to reign over us" It is precisely because the Son of God, when He came, established a kingdom upon earth, that therefore, in every land, in even nation, the Catholic Church governs with the authority of the universal Church of God. For instance, in England, the little and despised flock of Catholics united together under a hierarchy of ten years old, resting upon the Holy See as its centre, speaks and governs with a sovereignty derived from the whole Church of God. Therefore it is that ten years back the atmosphere was rent and tormented by the uproar of "Papal aggression." The natural instinct of the civil rulers knew that it was not a mere Christian philosophy wafted from foreign lands, but a government, a power, and a sovereignty. For this reason also, the extreme liberal school—those who claim toleration for every form of opinion, and who teach that the office of the civil governor is never to enter into controversies of religion, but that all men should be left free in their belief, and the conscience of all men be at liberty before God— even they make one exception, and, in the strangest contradiction to all their principles, or, at least, their professions. maintain that as the Catholic Church is not only a form of doctrine, but also a power or government, it must be excepted from the general toleration. And this is precisely the point of future collision. It is the very reason why the Archbishops of Cologne, Turin, Cagliari, and the like, went the other day into exile; why nineteen Sees are, at this moment, vacant in Sardinia. Why, in Italy, Bishops are, at this day, cast out from their Episcopal thrones: it is for this reason that in this land the Protestant religion is established instead of Catholic truth, and that thrones once filled by the Bishops of the universal Church are now occupied by those whom the royalties of England, and not the royalties of the Vicar of Jesus Christ, have chosen and set up. It is the same old contest, old as

Christianity itself, which has been from the beginning, first with pagan, and then with heretic, and then with schismatic, and then with infidel, and will continue to the end. The day is not far off, when the nations of the world, now so calm and peaceful in the stillness of their universal indifference, may easily be roused, and penal laws once more may be found in their Statute-books.

3. This leads on plainly to the marks which the prophet gives of the persecution of the last days. Now there are three things which he has recorded. In the foresight of prophecy he saw and noted these three signs. The first, that the continual sacrifice shall be taken away; the next, that the sanctuary shall be occupied by the abomination which maketh desolate; the third, that "the strength" and "the stars," as he described it: shall be cast down: and these are the only three I will notice.

Now, first of all what is this "taking away of the continual sacrifice"?

It was taken away in type at the destruction of Jerusalem. The sacrifice of the Temple, that is, of the lamb, morning and evening, in the Temple of God, was entirely abolished with the destruction of the Temple itself. Now the Prophet Malachias says: "From the rising of the sun even to the going down, any name is great among the Gentiles; and in every place there is sacrifice, and there is offered to my name a clean oblation." This passage of the prophet has been interpreted by the Fathers of the Church. beginning with St. Irenaeus, St. Justin Martyr, and I know not how many besides, to be the sacrifice of the Holy Eucharist, the true Paschal lamb which came in the place of the type— namely, the sacrifice of Jesus Himself on Calvary renewed perpetually and continued for ever in the sacrifice on the altar. Now has that continual sacrifice been taken away? That which was typical of it in old days has been already taken away. But has the reality been taken away? The holy Fathers who have written upon the subject of Antichrist, and of these prophecies of Daniel, without a single exception, as far as I know, and they are the Fathers both of the East and of the West, the Greek and the Latin Church—all of them unanimously,—say that in the latter end of the world, during the reign of Antichrist, the holy sacrifice of the altar will cease. In the work on the end of the world, ascribed to St. Hippolytus, after a long description of the afflictions of the last days, we read as follows: "The Churches shall lament with a great lamentation, for there shall be offered no more oblation, nor incense, nor worship acceptable to God. The sacred buildings of the churches shall be as hovels; and the precious body and blood of Christ shall not be manifest in those days; the Liturgy shall be extinct; the chanting of psalms shall cease; the reading of Holy Scripture shall be heard no more. But there shall be upon men darkness, and mourning upon mourning, and woe upon woe. Then, the Church shall be scattered, driven into the wilderness, and shall be for a time, as it was in the beginning, invisible, hidden in catacombs, in dens, in mountains, in lurking-places; for a time it shall be swept, as it were, from the face of the earth. Such is the universal testimony of the Fathers of the early centuries. Has there ever come to pass anything which may be called an installment or a forerunner of such an event as this? Look into the East. Mahometan superstition, which arose in Arabia, swept over Palestine and Asia Minor, the Seven Churches, and Egypt, the north of Africa—the home of St. Augustine, St. Cyprian, St. Optatus—and finally penetrated into Constantinople, soon it became dominant, has in every place persecuted and suppressed the worship and sacrifices of Jesus Christ. The Mahometan superstition at moment holds for its mosques a multitude of Christian churches, in which the continual sacrifice is already taken away, and the altar utterly destroyed. In Alexandria and in Constantinople there stand churches built for Christian worship, into which the foot of no Christian has ever entered since the continual sacrifice has been swept away. Surely in this we see, in part at least, the fulfilment of this prophecy; so much so, that many interpreters will have it that Mahomet is the Antichrist, and that none other is to come. No doubt he was one of the many forerunners and types of the Antichrist that shall be. Now let us look into the Western world: has the continual sacrifice been taken away in any other land? —for instance, in all those churches of Protestant Germany which were once Catholic, where the holy sacrifice of the Mass was daily offered! — throughout Norway, and Sweden, and Denmark, and one half of Switzerland, where there are a multitude of ancient Catholic churches — through England, in the cathedrals and the parish churches of this land, which were built simply as shrines of Jesus incarnate in the Holy Eucharist, as sanctuaries raised for the offering of the Holy Sacrifice? What is the characteristic mark of the Reformation, but the rejection of the Mass, and all that belongs to it, as declared in the Thirty-nine Articles of the

Church of England to be blasphemous fables and dangerous deceits? The suppression of the continual sacrifice is, above all, the mark and characteristic of the Protestant Reformation. We find, then, that this prophecy of Daniel has already its fulfilment both the East and West,— in the two wings, as it were while in the heart of Christendom the Holy Sacrifice is offered still. What is the great flood of infidelity, revolution, and anarchy, which is now sapping the foundations of Christian society, not only in France, but in Italy, and encompassing Rome, the centre and sanctuary of the Catholic Church, but the abomination which desolates the sanctuary, and takes away the continual sacrifice? The secret societies have long ago undermined and honeycombed the Christian society of Europe, and are at this moment struggling onward toward, Rome, the centre of all Christian order in the world. The fulfilment of the prophecy is yet to come; and that which we have seen in the two wings, we shall see also in the centre; and that great army of the Church of God will, for a time, be scattered. It will seem, for a while, to be defeated, and the power of the enemies of the faith for a time to prevail. The continual sacrifice will be taken away, and the sanctuary will be cast down. What can be more literally the abomination which makes desolate than the heresy which has removed the presence of the living God from the altar? [7] If you would understand this prophecy of desolation, enter into a church: which was once Catholic, where now is no sign of life; it stands empty, untenanted, without altar, without tabernacle, without the presence of Jesus. And that which has already come to pass in the East and in the West is extending itself throughout the centre of the Catholic unity.

The Protestant spirit of England, and the schismatical spirit even of countries Catholic in name. is at this moment urging on the great anticatholic movement of Italy. Hostility to the Holy See is the true and governing motive. And thus we come to the third mark, the casting down of "the Prince of Strength;" that is, the Divine authority

---

[7] Saint Alphonsus says: "Hence St. Bonaventure says that in the Mass God manifest to us all the love that He has borne us, and includes in it, as in a compendium, all His benefits. On this account the Devil has always endeavored to abolish the Mass throughout the world by means of heretics, making them the precursors of Antichrist who, before all things, will endeavor to abolish, and in fact will, in punishment for the sins of men, succeed in abolishing the Holy Sacrifice of the Altar, according to the prediction of Daniel: 'And strength was given him against the continual sacrifice because of sins.'"

of the Church, and especially of him in whose person it is embodied, the Vicar of Jesus Christ. God has invested him with sovereignty, and given to him a home and a patrimony on earth. The world is in arms to depose him, and to leave him no place to lay his head. Rome and the Roman States are the inheritance of the Incarnation. The world is resolved to drive the Incarnation off the earth. It will not suffer it to possess so much as to set the sole of its foot upon. This is the true interpretation of the anticatholic movement of Italy and England: "Tolle hunc de terra." The dethronement of the Vicar of Christ is the dethronement of the hierarchy of the universal Church, and the public rejection of the Presence and Reign of Jesus.

4. Nor, if I am obliged to enter somewhat into the future, I shall confine myself to tracing out very general outline. The direct tendency of all the events we see at this moment is clearly this, to overthrow Catholic worship throughout the world. Already we see that every Government in Europe is excluding religion from its public acts. The civil powers are desecrating themselves: government is without religion; and if government be without religion, education must be without religion. We see it already in Germany and in France. It has been again and again attempted in England. The result of this can be nothing but the re-establishment of mere natural society; that is to say, the governments and the powers of the world, which for a time were subdued by the Church of God to a belief in Christianity, to obedience to the laws of God, and to the unity of the Church, having revolted from it and desecrated themselves, hare relapsed into their natural state

The Prophet Daniel, in the twelfth chapter, says that in the time of the end "many shall be chosen and made white, and shall be tried as fire; and the wicked shall deal wickedly, and none of the wicked shall understand, but the learned shall understand;" that is, many who have known the faith shall abandon it, by apostasy. "Some of the learned shall fall;" (Daniel 11:33) that is, they shall fall from their fidelity to God. And how shall this come to pass? Firstly by fear, partly by deception, partly by cowardice, partly because they cannot stand for unpopular truth in the face of popular falsehood; partly because the overruling contemptuous public opinion, as in such country as this, and in France, so subdues and frightens Catholics, that they dare not avow their principles, and, at last, dare not hold them. They become admirers and worshipers of the material prosperity of Protestant countries. They see the commerce, the manufacture, the agriculture, the capital, the practical science, the irresistible armies, and the fleets that cover the sea, and they come flocking to adore, and say, "Nothing is so great as this great country of Protestant England." And so they give up their faith, and become materialists, seeking for the wealth and power of this world, dazzled and overpowered by the greatness of a country which has cast off its fidelity to the Church.

5. Now the last result of all this will be a persecution, which I will not attempt to describe. It is enough to remind you of the words of our Divine Master: "Brother shall betray brother to death:" it shall be a persecution in which no man shall spare his neighbour, in which the powers of the world will wreak upon the Church of God such a revenge as the world before has never known. The Word of God tells us that towards the end of time the power of this world will became so irresistible and so triumphant that the Church of God will sink underneath its hand — that the Church of God will receive no more help from emperors, or kings, or princes, or legislatures, or nations, or peoples, to make resistance against the power and the might of its antagonist. It will be deprived of protection. It will be weakened, baffled, and prostrate, and will lie bleeding at the feet of the powers of this world. Does this seem incredible? What, then, do we see at this moment? Look at the Catholic and Roman Church throughout the world. When was it ever more like its Divine Head in the hour when He was bound hand and foot by those who betrayed Him? Look at the Catholic Church, still independent, faithful to its Divine trust, and yet cast off by the nations of the world; at the Holy Father, the Vicar of our Divine Lord, at this moment mocked, scorned, despised, betrayed, abandoned, robbed of his own, and even those that would defend him murdered. When, I ask, was the Church of God ever in a weaker condition, in a feebler state in the eyes of men, and in this natural order, than it is now? And from whence, I ask, is deliverance to come? Is there on earth any power to intervene? Is there any king, prince, or potentate, that has the power to interpose either his will or his sword for the protection of the Church? Not one; and it is foretold it should be so. Neither need we desire it, for the will of God seems to be otherwise. But there is One Power which will destroy all antagonists; there is One Person who will break down and smite small as the dust of the summer threshing-floor all the enemies of the Church, for it is He who will

consume His enemies "with the Spirit of His mouth," and destroy them "with the brightness of His coming." It seems as if the Son of God were jealous lest any one should vindicate His authority. He has claimed the battle to Himself; He has taken up the gage which has been cast down against Him; and prophecy is plain and explicit that the last overthrow of evil will be His; that it will be wrought by no man, but by the Son of God; that all the nations of the world may know that He, and He alone, is King, and that He, and He alone, is God. We read in the Book Apocalypse of the city of Rome, that she said in the pride of her heart, "I sit as a queen, and am no widow, and sorrow I shall not see. Therefore shall her plagues come in one day, death, and mourning, and famine, and she shall be burned with the fire, because God is strong who shall judge her." Some of the greatest writers of the Church tell us that in all probability, in the last overthrow of the enemies of God, the city of Rome itself will he destroyed; it will be a second time punished by Almighty God, as it was in the beginning. There was never destruction upon earth comparable to the overthrow of Rome in ancient days. St. Gregory the Great, writing of it, says, "Rome a little while ago was seen to be the mistress of the world; what she now is we behold. Crushed by manifold and boundless miseries, by the desolation of her inhabitants, the inroads of enemies, the frequency of destruction, we set fulfilled in her the words of the Prophet against the city. Where is the senate; where now is the people? The bones are decayed, and the flesh is consumed. All the pomp of worldly greatness in her is extinguished. Her whole structure is dissolved. And we, the few who remain, are day by day harassed by the sword and by innumerable tribulations. Rome is empty and burning; ... her people have failed, and even her walls are falling ... Where now are they who once exulted in her glory? Where is their pomp; where their pride; where their constant and immoderate rejoicing?" There never was a ruin like to the overthrow of the great City of the Seven Hills, when the words of the prophecy were fulfilled: "Babylon is fallen"—like "a great millstone cast into the sea"

The writers of the Church tell us that in the latter days the city of Rome will probably become apostate from the Church and Vicar of Jesus Christ; and that Rome will again be punished, for he will depart from it; and the judgment of God will fall on the place from which he once reigned over the nations of the world. For what is it that makes

Rome sacred, but the presence of the Vicar of Jesus Christ? What has it that should be dear in the sight of God, save only the presence of the Vicar of His Son? Let the Church of Christ depart from Rome, and Rome will be no more in the eye of God than Jerusalem of old. Jerusalem, the Holy City, chosen by God, was cast down and consumed by fire, because it crucified the Lord of Glory; and the city of Rome, which has been the seat of the Vicar of Jesus Christ for eighteen hundred years, if it become apostate, like Jerusalem of old, will suffer a like condemnation. And, therefore, the writers of the Church tell us that the city of Rome has no prerogative except only that the Vicar of Christ is there; and if it become unfaithful, the same judgments which fell on Jerusalem, hallowed though it was by the presence of the Son of God, of the Master, and not the disciple only, shall fall likewise upon Rome.

The apostasy of the city of Rome from the Vicar of Christ, and its destruction by Antichrist, may be thoughts so new to many Catholics, that I think it well to recite the text of theologians in the greatest repute. First, Malvenda, who writes expressly on the subject, states as the opinion of Ribera, Gaspar Melus, Viegas, Suarez, Bellarmine and Bosius, that Rome shall apostatise from the faith and drive away the Vicar of Christ, and return to its ancient paganism. Malvenda's words are: "Rome itself in the last times of the world will return to its ancient idolatry, power, and imperial greatness. It will cast out its Pontiff, altogether apostatise from the Christian faith, terribly persecute the Church, shed the blood of martyrs more cruelly than ever, and will recover its former state of abundant wealth, or even greater than it had under its first rulers."

Lessius says: "In the time of Antichrist, Rome shall be destroyed, as we see openly from the thirteenth chapter of the Apocalypse;" and again: "The woman whom thou sawest is the great city, which hath kingdom over the kings of the earth, in which is signified Rome in its impiety, such as it "as in time of St. John, and shall be again at the end of the world." And Bellarmine "In the time of Antichrist, Rome shall be desolated and burnt, as ye learn from the sixteenth verse of the seventeenth chapter of the Apocalypse." On which words the Jesuit Erbermann comments as follows: "We all confess with Bellarmine that the Roman people, a little before the end of the world, will return to Paganism, and drive out the Roman Pontiff."

Viegas, on the eighteenth chapter of the Apocalypse, says: "Rome, in the last age of the world, after it has apostatised from the faith, will attain to great power and splendour of wealth, and its sway will he widely spread throughout the world, and flourish greatly. Living in luxury and the abundance of all things, it will worship idols, and be steeped in all kinds of superstition, and will pay honeur to false gods. And because of the vast effusion of the blood of martyrs which war shed under the emperors, God will most severely and justly avenge them, and it shall be utterly destroyed, and burned by a most terrible and afflicting conflagration."

Finally, Cornelius A. Lapide sums up what may be said to be the common interpretation of theologians. Commenting on the same eighteenth chapter of the Apocalypse, he says: "These things are to be understood of the city of Rome, not that which is, nor that which was, but that which shall ho at the end of the world. For then the city of Rome will return to its former glory, and likewise its idolatry and other sins, and shall be such as it was in the time of St. John, under Nero, Domitian, Decius, etc. For from Christian it shall again become heathen. It shall cast out the Christian Pontiff, and the faithful who adhere to him. It shall persecute and slay them. It shall rival the persecutions of the heathen emperors against the Christians. . . . . For so we see Jerusalem was first heathen under the Canaanite; secondly, faithful under the Jews; thirdly, Christian under the Apostles; fourthly, heathen again under the Romans; fifthly, Saracen under the Turks."

Such they believe will be the history of Rome: pagan under the emperors, Christian under the Apostles, faithful under the Pontiffs, apostate under the Revolution, and pagan under Antichrist. Only Jerusalem could sin so formally and fall so low; for only Jerusalem has been so chosen, illumined, and consecrated. And as no people were ever so intense, in their persecutions of Jesus as the Jews, so I fear will none ever be more relentless against the fair than the Romans.

Now I have not attempted to point out what shall be the future events except in outline, and I have never ventured to designate who shall be the person who shall accomplish them. Of this I know nothing; but I am enabled with the most perfect certainty, from the Word of God, and from the interpretations of the Church, to point out the great principles which are in conflict on either side I began by showing you that the Antichrist, and the antichristian movement, has these marks:

first, schism from the Church of God; secondly, denial of its Divine and infallible voice; and thirdly, denial of the Incarnation. It is, therefore, the direct and mortal enemy of the One Holy Catholic and Roman Church—the unity from which all schism is made; the sole organ of the Divine voice of the Spirit of God; the shrine and sanctuary of the Incarnation and of the continual sacrifice.

And now to make an end. Men have need to look to their principles. They have to make a choice between two things, between faith in a teacher speaking with an infallible voice, governing the unity which now, as in the beginning, knits together the nations of the world, or the spirit of fragmentary Christianity, which is the source of disorder and ends in unbelief. Here is the simple choice which we are all brought; and between them we must make up our minds.

The events of every day are carrying men further and further in the career on which they have entered. Every day men are becoming more and more divided. These are times of sifting. Our Divine Lord is standing in the Church: "His fan is in His hand, and He will thoroughly cleanse His and He will gather the grain into His barn, and will burn up the chaff with unquenchable fire." It is a time of trial, when "some of the learned shall fall," and those only shall be saved who is steadfast to the end. The two great antagonists are gathering their forces for the last conflict;—it may not be in our day, it may not be in the time of those who come after us; but one thing is certain, that we are as much put on our trial now as they will he who live in the time when it shall come to pass. For as surely as the Son of God reigns on high, and will reign "until He has put all His enemies under His feet," so surely every one that lifts a heel or directs a weapon against His faith, His Church, or His Vicar car upon earth, will share the judgment which is laid up for the Antichrist whom he serves.

Antichrist

Biblical Marks of Antichrist

1. "Who is a liar, but he who denies that Jesus is the Christ? This is Antichrist, who denies the Father and the Son." I John 18:22
2. II Thessalonians 2:4 "Who opposeth and is lifted up above all that is called God or that is worshipped, so that he sitteth in the temple of God, shewing himself as if he were God."
3. II Thessalonians 2:9-10 "him whose coming is according to the working of Satan, in all power, and signs, and lying wonders: and in all seduction of iniquity to them that perish: because they receive not the love of the truth, that they might be saved." Saint Augustine (De Civ. Dei, xx. 19): "It is a matter of debate whether they are called signs and lying wonders, because he will deceive the senses of mortals, by imaginary visions, in that he will seem to do what he does not, or because. though they be real wonders, they will seduce into falsehood them that believe."
4. Daniel 7:21 "I beheld, and lo, that horn made war against the saints and prevailed over them. ... And he will speak words against the High One and shall crush the saints of the most High."
5. Daniel 7:25 "And he shall think himself able to change times and laws: and they shall be delivered into his hands until a time and times and half a time."
6. Daniel 8:11-12: "And it was magnified even to the prince of strength: and it took away from him the continual sacrifice and cast down the place of his sanctuary. And strength was given him against he continual sacrifice because of sins: and truth shall be cast down on the ground, and he shall do and shall prosper."
7. Daniel 11:30-31,36: "And the galley and the Romans shall come upon him: and he shall be struck and shall return and shall have indignation against the covenant of the sanctuary. And he shall succeed: and he shall return and shell devise against them that have forsaken the covenant of

the sanctuary. And arms shall stand on his part and they shall defile the sanctuary of strength and shall take away the continual sacrifice: and they shall place there the abomination of desolation. ... And the king shall do according to his will, and he shall be lifted up and shall magnify himself against every god: and he shall speak great things against the God of gods and shall prosper till the wrath be accomplished. For the determination is made."

8. John 17:12: "While I was with them, I kept them in thy name. Those whom thou gavest me have I kept: and none of them is lost, but the son of perdition: that the scripture may be fulfilled."

9. John 5:43 "I am come in the name of my Father, and you receive me not: if another shall come in his own name, him you will receive."

10. "Little children, it is the last hour: and as you have heard that Antichrist cometh, even now there are become many Antichrists: whereby we know that it is the last hour. They went out from us but they were not of us. For if they had been of us, they would no doubt have remained with us: but that they may be manifest, that they are not all of us." I John 2:18-19

SAINT GREGORY VII "We, therefore, who are bound, by our position, to destroy vice and implant virtue in the hearts of our brethren, we pray and beseech you, in the Lord Jesus who redeemed us, that you would consider within yourselves, and understand why it is that we have to suffer such anguish and tribulation from the enemies of the Christian religion. From the day when, by the Divine will, the Mother-Church, despite my great unworthiness, and (as God is my witness) despite my own wish, placed me on the Apostolic Throne, the one object of all my labours has been that the Spouse of God, our Mistress and Mother, should recover her just rights, in order that she may be free, chaste and Catholic. But such a line of conduct must have caused extreme displeasure to the old enemy; and therefore has he marshalled against us them that are his members, and has stirred up against us a world-wide opposition. Hence it is that there have been used against us, and against the Apostolic See, efforts of a more violent character than any that have ever been attempted since the days of Constantine the Great. But there is nothing surprising in all this: it is but natural that the nearer we approach to the time of Antichrist,, the more furious will be the attempts to annihilate the Christian religion.""

Culleton: <u>Prophets and Our Times</u>, page 25: "After the birth of Anti-Christ and shortly before the rise of the Great Monarch, the false doctrines were to multiply and spread to such an extent that even Catholics would doubt many of the articles of faith, resulting in their perversion, this to apply not only tot he laity but even to many priests and some of the hierarchy. The zeal of these latter will be greatly affected by this lack of faith. There will be dissentions among the clergy. Many will be proud, selfish, unjust, covetous, and even forgetful of vows made at ordination regarding chastity. Many will even offer Mass and confer the Sacraments sacrilegiously."

Saint Louis de Montfort, <u>True Devotion to Mary</u> died 1716: "And, lastly, Mary must be terrible to the devil and his crew, as an army arranged in battle, principally in these latter times, because the devil, knowing that he has but little time, and now less than every, to destroy souls, will every day redouble his efforts and his combats. He will presently raise up new persecutions, and will put terrible snares before the faithful servants and true children of Mary, whom it gives him more trouble to surmount than it does to conquer others.

"It is primarily these last and cruel persecutions of the devil, which shall go on increasing daily until the reign of Antichrist, that we ought to understand that first and celebrated prediction of God, pronounced in the terrestrial Paradise against the serpent. It is to our purpose to explain this here, for the glory of the most holy Virgin, for the salvation of her children, and for the confusion of the devil.

Dom Gueranger states on the Feast of Saint Stephen: "From the murder of the innocent Abel to the future Martyrs who are to shed their blood in the days of Anti-christ, the Church is always under persecution; in some country she is ever shedding her blood; but her strength lies in her fidelity to Jesus her Spouse, and in the simplicity which the Babe of Bethlehem is come to teach her by His own example."

Saint Hilary on Antichrist

The time for speaking is come, the time for silence is past. Let Christ now appear, for Antichrist has begun his reign. Let the Shepherds give the alarm, for the hirelings have fled. Let us lay down our lives for our sheep, for thieves have got into the fold, and a furious lion is prowling around it. Let us prepare for martyrdom. ... for the angel of satan hath transformed himself into an angel of light.

'Why, O my God, didst thou not permit me to confess thy holy Name, and be the minister of Thine Only Begotten Son, in the times of Nero or Decius? Full of the fire of the Holy Ghost, I would not have feared the rack, for I would have thought of Isaias, how he was sawn in two. I would not have feared fire, for I would have said to myself that the Hebrew Children sang in their fiery furnace. The cross and the breaking of every bone of my body should not have made me a coward, for the good thief would have encouraged me, who was translated into thy kingdom. If they had threatened to drown me in the angry billows of the deep ocean, I would have laughed at their threats, for thou hast taught us, by the example of Jonas and Paul, that thou canst give life to thy servants even in the sea.

'Happy I, could I thus have fought with men who professed themselves to be the enemies of thy name; every one would have said that they who had recourse to tortures, and sword, and fire, to compel a Christian to deny thee, were persecutors; and my death would have been sufficient testimony to thy truth, O God! The battle would have been an open one, and no one would have hesitated to call by the honest name these men that denied thee, and racked and murdered us; and thy people, seeing that it was an evident persecution, would have followed their Pastors in the confession of their faith.

'But nowadays, we have to do with a disguised persecutor, a smooth-tongued enemy, a Constantius who has put on Antichrist; who scourges us, not with lashes, but with caresses who instead of robbing us, which would give us spiritual life, bribes us with riches, that he may lead us to eternal death; who thrusts us not into the liberty of a prison, but into the honours of his palace, that he may enslave us: who tears not our flesh, but our hearts; who beheads not with a sword, but kills the soul with his gold; who sentences not by a herald that we are to be burnt, but covertly enkindles the fire of hell against us. He does not dispute with us, that he may conquer; but he flatters us, that so he may lord it over our souls. He confesses Christ, the better to deny Him; he tries to procure a unity which shall destroy peace; he puts down some few heretics, so that he may also crush the Christians; he honours Bishops, that they may cease to be Bishops; he builds up Churches, that he may pull down the Faith.

'Let men talk as they will, and accuse me of strong language, and calumny: it is. the duty of a minister of the truth to speak the truth. If what I say be untrue, let me be branded with the name of an infamous calumniator: but if I prove what I assert, then I am not exceeding the bounds of apostolic liberty, nor transgressing the humility of a successor of the Apostles by speaking thus, after so long observing silence. . . No, this is not rashness, it is faith; it is not inconsiderateness, it is duty; it is not passion, it is conscience.

'I say to thee, Constantius, what I would have said to Nero, or Decius, or Maximian: You are fighting against God, you are raging against the Church, you are persecuting the saints, you are hating the preachers of Christ, you are destroying religion, you are a tyrant, not in human things, but in things that appertain to God. Yes, this is what I should say to thee as well as to them; but listen, now, to what can only be said to thyself: Thou falsely callest thyself a Christian, for thou art a new enemy of Christ; thou art a precursor of Antichrist, and a doer of his mystery of iniquity; thou, that art a rebel to the faith, art making formulas of faith; thou art intruding thine own creatures into the sees of the Bishops; thou art putting out the good and putting in the bad. ... By a strange ingenious plan, which no one had ever yet discovered, thou hast found a way to persecute, without making Martyrs.

'We owe much to you, Nero, Decius, and Maximian! your cruelty did us service. We conquered the devil by your persecutions. The blood of the holy Martyrs you made has been treasured up throughout the world, and their venerable relics are ever strengthening us in faith by their mute unceasing testimony. . . . . But thou, Constantius, cruel with thy refinement of cruelty, art an enemy that ragest against us, doing us more injury, and leaving us less hope of pardon.... Thou deprivest the fallen of the excuse they might have had with their Eternal Judge, when they showed him the scars and wounds they had endured for him, for perhaps their tortures might induce him to forgive their weakness. Whereas thou, most wicked of men! thou hast invented a persecution which, if we fall, robs us of pardon, and, if we triumph, does not make us Martyrs!

We see thee, ravenous wolf, under thy sheep's clothing. Thou adornest the sanctuaries of God's temples with the gold of the State, and thou offerest to him what is taken from the temples, or taxed by edict, or extorted by penalty. Thou receivest his Priests with a kiss like that which betrayed Christ. Thou bowest down thy head for a blessing, and then thou tramplest on our Faith. Thou dispensest the clergy from paying tributes and taxes to Caesar, that thou mayest bribe them to be renegades to Christ, foregoing thy own rights, that God may be deprived of his!'

Saint Irenaeus

1. And not only by the particulars already mentioned, but also by means of the events which shall occur in the time of Antichrist is it shown that he, being an apostate and a robber, is anxious to be adored as God; and that, although a mere slave, he wishes himself to be proclaimed as a king. For he (Antichrist) being endued with all the power of the devil, shall come, not as a righteous king, nor as a legitimate king, [i.e., one] in subjection to God, but an impious, unjust, and lawless one; as an apostate, iniquitous and murderous; as a robber, concentrating in himself [all] satanic apostasy, and setting aside idols to persuade [men] that he himself is God, raising up himself as the only idol, having in himself the multifarious errors of the other idols. This he does, in order that they who do [now] worship the devil by means of many abominations, may serve himself by this one idol, of whom the apostle thus speaks in the second Epistle to the Thessalonians: "Unless there shall come a failing away first, and the man of sin shall be revealed, the son of perdition, who opposeth and exalteth himself above all that is called God, or that is worshipped; so that he sitteth in the temple of God, showing himself as if he were God." The apostle therefore clearly points out his apostasy, and that he is lifted up above all that is called God, or that is worshipped--that is, above every idol-- for these are indeed so called by men, but are not [really] gods; and that he will endeavour in a tyrannical manner to set himself forth as God.

2. Moreover, he (the apostle) has also pointed out this which I have shown in many ways, that the temple in Jerusalem was made by

the direction of the true God. For the apostle himself, speaking in his own person, distinctly called it the temple of God. Now I have shown in the third book, that no one is termed God by the apostles when speaking for themselves, except Him who truly is God, the Father of our Lord, by whose directions the temple which is at Jerusalem was constructed for those purposes which I have already mentioned; in which [temple] the enemy shall sit, endeavouring to show himself as Christ, as the Lord also declares: "But when ye shall see the abomination of desolation, which has been spoken of by Daniel the prophet, standing in the holy place (let him that readeth understand), then let those who are in Judea flee into the mountains; and he who is upon the house-top, let him not come down to take anything out of his house: for there shall then be great hardship, such as has not been from the beginning of the world until now, nor ever shall be."

3. Daniel too, looking forward to the end of the last kingdom, i.e., the ten last kings, amongst whom the kingdom of those men shall be partitioned, and upon whom the son of perdition shall come, declares that ten horns shall spring from the beast, and that another little horn shall arise in the midst of them, and that three of the former shall be rooted up before his face. He says: "And, behold, eyes were in this horn as the eyes of a man, and a mouth speaking great things, and his look was more stout than his fellows. I was looking, and this horn made war against the saints, and prevailed against them, until the Ancient of days came and gave judgment to the saints of the most high God, and the time came, and the saints obtained the kingdom." Then, further on, in the interpretation of the vision, there was said to him: "The fourth beast shall be the fourth kingdom upon earth, which shall excel all other kingdoms, and devour the whole earth, and tread it down, and cut it in pieces. And its ten horns are ten kings which shall arise; and after them shall arise another, who shall surpass in evil deeds all that were before him, and shall overthrow three kings; and he shall speak words against the most high God, and wear out the saints of the most high God, and shall purpose to change times and laws; and [everything] shall be given into his hand until a time of times and a half time," that is, for three years and six months, during which time, when he comes, he shall reign over the earth. Of whom also the Apostle Paul again, speaking in the second [Epistle] to the Thessalonians, and at the same time proclaiming the cause of his advent, thus says: "And then

48

shall the wicked one be revealed, whom the Lord Jesus shall slay with the spirit of His mouth, and destroy by the presence of His coming; whose coming [i.e., the wicked one's] is after the working of Satan, in all power, and signs, and portents of lies, and with all deceivableness of wickedness for those who perish; because they did not receive the love of the truth, that they might be saved. And therefore God will send them the working of error, that they may believe a lie; that they all may be judged who did not believe the truth, but gave consent to iniquity,"

4. The Lord also spoke as follows to those who did not believe in Him: "I have come in my Father's name, and ye have not received Me: when another shall come in his own name, him ye will receive," calling Antichrist "the other," because he is alienated from the Lord. This is also the unjust judge, whom the Lord mentioned as one "who feared not God, neither regarded man," to whom the widow fled in her forgetfulness of God,--that is, the earthly Jerusalem,--to be avenged of her adversary. Which also he shall do in the time of his kingdom: he shall remove his kingdom into that [city], and shall sit in the temple of God, leading astray those who worship him, as if he were Christ. To this purpose Daniel says again: "And he shall desolate the holy place; and sin has been given for a sacrifice, and righteousness been cast away in the earth, and he has been active (fecit), and gone on prosperously." And the angel Gabriel, when explaining his vision, states with regard to this person: "And towards the end of their kingdom a king of a most fierce countenance shall arise, one understanding [dark] questions, and exceedingly powerful, full of wonders; and he shall corrupt, direct, influence (faciet), and put strong men down, the holy people likewise; and his yoke shall be directed as a wreath [round their neck]; deceit shall be in his hand, and he shall be lifted up in his heart: he shall also ruin many by deceit, and lead many to perdition, bruising them in his hand like eggs." And then he points out the time that his tyranny shall last, during which the saints shall be put to flight, they who offer a pure sacrifice unto God: "And in the midst of the week," he says, "the sacrifice and the libation shall be taken away, and the abomination of desolation [shall be brought] into the temple: even unto the consummation of the time shall the desolation be complete." Now three years and six months constitute the half-week.

49

5. From all these passages are revealed to us, not merely the particulars of the apostasy, and [the doings] of him who concentrates in himself every satanic error, but also, that there is one and the same God the Father, who was declared by the prophets, but made manifest by Christ. For if what Daniel prophesied concerning the end has been confirmed by the Lord, when He said, "When ye shall see the abomination of desolation, which has been spoken of by Daniel the prophet" (and the angel Gabriel gave the interpretation of the visions to Daniel, and he is the archangel of the Creator (Demiurgi), who also proclaimed to Mary the visible coining and the incarnation of Christ), then one and the same God is most manifestly pointed out, who sent the prophets, and made promise of the Son, and called us into His knowledge.

Frederick William Faber (d. 1863)

a. "From the first, all the troubles of the Church were regarded as types of Antichrist, as Christ had His types; so we naturally conclude with this. It is not an idle speculation ; Scripture puts it before us.

b. The person of Antichrist.

1. A single person. The man of sin, the son of perdition, that wicked one.' (2 Thess. 2: 3) This is Antichrist, who denieth the Father and the Son/ (1 John 2:22)

2. Many believed in a demoniacal incarnation — this will not be so — but he will be a man utterly possessed. (Card. Berulle.)

3. Not come yet — Mahomet was not he — the signs are not fulfilled.

4. He is to be a king — his kingdom in visible antagonism to the kingdom of Christ — so all civil oppositions have been precursors of Antichrist.

5. Certainly a Jew — uncertain if of tribe of Dan — origin probably obscure.

6. With zeal for the temple, gives himself out as the Messias.

7. With immense talents, awfully assisted by the devil — immense wealth, Dan. xi — immoral, Dan vii.; and xi. unparalleled in deceit — deceiving even the elect.

8. His doctrine an apparent contradiction of no religion, yet a new religion. Comparison with French Revolution. (1) He denies the

divinity of Christ. (2) Asserts that he is the Messias. (3) Worship of devils. (4) He is an atheist, (5) but begins by affecting respect for the law of Moses. (6) Lying miracles, false resurrection, mock ascension. (7) He has an attendant pontiff so separating regal and prophetic office.

c. His kingdom.

1. Not hereditary — got by degrees, by fraud, talent, and iniquitous diplomacy.

2. It will begin at Babylon. (Zach. v. 11.)

3. It will extend in influence over the whole civilized world.

4. Jerusalem will be the metropolis.

5. When his empire is at its full, it will last only three years and a half.

d. His persecution.

1. Unparalleled horror of it. (Apoc. xx.)

2. In spiritual things — (1) there will be hardly any mass, (2) but the worship of his image and the wearing of his mark; (3) Majority of Christians will apostatize, (4) but the Church will not be destroyed.

3. Saints will be greater than ever — martyrs greater, as the first fought against men, the latter will fight against devils, our Lady's Saints, vide Grignon de Montfort.

4. Enoch and Elias, new confirmed in grace, and waiting — they will preach in sackcloth — for as long a time as Christ, i.e. three years and a half less nineteen days — their martyrdom — they will lie unburied.

5. Jesus kills him, and comes to the doom forty-five days after ; some say that St. Michael will kill him on Mount Olivet.

e. Protestantism an anticipation of Antichrist.

(1) Its attitude towards the Blessed Virgin Mary, (2) the Mass, (3) sign of the cross. (4) All its sects unite against the Church. (5) Its carelessness about Baptism; sixth angel drying up Euphrates. (6) It blasphemes Saints.

f. The Five-and-Forty Days.

(1) Space for repentance. (2) Full of signs. (3) The Lord comes and the weary world is judged and burnt.

g. Lessons.

1. The reign of Antichrist is to be the last temporal reign: so the Church's last enemy is to be a kingdom, the con- summation of the wickedness of all kingdoms; how significant!

2. What part should we take in this persecution? Let us measure it by the boldness of our profession now — by our strictness with ourselves — by our self-denial in charity for others — by our perseverance in the practices of penance — by the fervor and the frequency of our prayers — by the rigorousness cf the examinations of our conscience. It is always to each of us the five-and-forty days; Christ will come — He will not tarry — let us have our loins girded and our lamps burning, that when the midnight cry is raised, and the Bridegroom cometh, we may go forward with holy awe to meet our Saviour and our Judge."

The Holy Sacrifice of the Mass Fails

Daniel

"And it was magnified even to their prince of the strength: and it took away from him the continual sacrifice, and cast down the place of his sanctuary. And strength was given him against the continual sacrifice, because of sins: and truth shall be cast down on the ground, and he shall do and shall prosper. And I heard one of the saints speaking, and one saint said to another, I know not to whom that was speaking: How long shall be the vision, concerning the continual sacrifice, and the sin of the desolation that is made: and the sanctuary, and the strength be trodden under foot? And he said to him: Unto evening and morning two thousand three hundred days: and the sanctuary shall be cleansed. [8]

"And arms shall stand on his part, and they shall defile the sanctuary of strength, and shall take away the continual sacrifice, and they shall place there the abomination unto desolation. [9]

"And he shall confirm the covenant with many, in one week: and in the half of the week the victim and the sacrifice shall fail: and there shall be in the temple the abomination of desolation: and the desolation shall continue even to the consummation, and to the end. [10]

"And from the time when the continual sacrifice shall be taken away, and the abomination unto desolation shall be set up, there shall be a thousand two hundred ninety days. Blessed is he that waiteth, and cometh unto a thousand three hundred thirty-five days. [11]

"And he said to him: Unto evening and morning two thousand three hundred days: and the sanctuary shall be cleansed." [12]

Joel: "Between the porch and the altar the priests the Lord's ministers shall weep, and shall say: Spare, O Lord, spare thy people: and give not thy inheritance to reproach, that the heathen should rule over them. Why should they say among the nations: Where is their God?" [13]

---

[8] Daniel 8:11-14
[9] Daniel 11:31
[10] Daniel 9:27
[11] Daniel 12:11-12
[12] Daniel 8:14
[13] Joel 2:17

Osee 3:4-5: "For the children of Israel shall sit many days without king, and without prince, and without sacrifice, and without altar, and without ephod, and without theraphim. And after this the children of Israel shall return, and shall seek the Lord their God, and David their king: and they shall fear the Lord, and his goodness in the last days." Judges 17:5 tells us that the theraphim is a priestly vestment: "And he separated also therein a little temple for the god, and made an ephod, and theraphim, that is to say, a priestly garment, and idols: and he filled the hand of one of his sons, and he became his priest."

Osee: "My people have been silent, because they had no knowledge: because thou hast rejected knowledge, I will reject thee, that thou shalt not do the office of priesthood to me: and thou hast forgotten the law of thy God, I also will forget thy children." [14]

Malachias: "For from the rising of the sun even to the going down, my name is great among the Gentiles, and in every place there is sacrifice, and there is offered to my name a clean oblation: for my name is great among the Gentiles, saith the Lord of hosts." [15]

Malachias "And you have profaned it in that you say: The table of the Lord is defiled: and that which is laid thereupon is contemptible with the fire that devoureth it." [16]

Matthew "When therefore you shall see the abomination of desolation, which was spoken of by Daniel the prophet, standing in the holy place: he that readeth let him understand. Then they that are in Judea, let them flee to the mountains: And he that is on the housetop, let him not come down to take any thing out of his house: And he that is in the field, let him not go back to take his coat." [17]

Apocalypse: "And they overcame him by the blood of the Lamb and by the word of the testimony: and they loved not their lives unto death." [18]

---

[14] Osee 4:6
[15] Malachias 1:11
[16] Malachias 1:12
[17] Matthew 24:15-18. It is recommended to read Matthew 24, Mark 13 and Luke 21
[18] Apocalypse 12:11

"I wish to celebrate Mass and confect the Body and Blood of our Lord Jesus Christ, according to the rite of the Holy Roman Church, to the praise of almighty God, of the whole triumphant Court of heaven, to my benefit and to the benefit of the whole Church militant, for all who have commended themselves to my prayers, both generally and specially, and for the favorable condition of the holy Roman Church. Amen." [19]

Saint Athanasius   (Died 373) "It is a fact that they have the churches, but you have the Apostolic Faith." said Saint Athanasius.

Saint Jerome (Died 420)

"The abomination of desolation can be taken to mean as well every perverted doctrine. When we see such a thing stand in the holy place, that is in the Church, and pretend that it is God, we must flee from Judea to the mountains, that is, departing from the letter of the law which kills, and from Jewish distortions of the law, we must draw near to the eternal mountains where God shines wondrously. We must be on a housetop and in a house where the fiery darts of the devil cannot reach us. We must not come down and carry with us anything from the house of our old manner of life, nor seek the things we left behind. Rather we are to sow in the field of the spiritual scriptures to read a harvest from them. Neither shall we take another cloak. Such things are forbidden Apostles."

Pope Saint Leo the Great (Died 461) "The priest who does not withdraw from error proves that he is himself involved in it." [20]

Saint Francis de Sales (Died 1622) "Is it not written that the revolt and separation must come (II Thessalonians 2:3), and that the sacrifice shall cease (Daniel 12:11), and that the Son of Man shall hardly find faith on earth at His second visible return (Luke 18:8), when He will come to judge? Answer: all these passages are understood of the affliction which antichrist will cause in the Church, during the three and a half years that he shall reign mightily; but in spite of this the Church during even these three years shall not fail, and shall be fed and

---

[19] From the Preparation for Mass reprinted in both the Missale Romanum and Breviarum Romanum as part of the preparation **prescribed** for priests.

[20] Saint Leo, quoted in Dignity and Duties of the Priest, page 180

preserved amid the deserts and solitudes whither is shall retire, as the Scripture says (Apocalypse 12)" [21]

Council of Trent: "Defects may arise in respect to the formula, if anything is wanting to complete the actual words of consecration. The words of consecration, which are the formative principle of this sacrament, are as follows:
"FOR THIS IS MY BODY and
"FOR THIS IS THE CHALICE OF MY BLOOD OF THE NEW AND EVERLASTING COVENANT, THE MYSTERY OF FAITH, WHICH SHALL BE SHED FOR YOU AND FOR MANY UNTO THE REMISSION OF SINS
"If any omission or alteration is made in the formula of consecration of the Body and Blood, involving a change of meaning, the consecration is invalid. An addition made without altering the meaning does not invalidate the consecration, but the celebrant commits a mortal sin."

The Catechism of the Council of Trent says: "With reason, therefore, were the words for all not used, as in this place the fruits of the Passion are alone spoken of, and to the elect only did His Passion bring the fruit of salvation. And this is the purport of the Apostle when he says: Christ was offered once to exhaust the sins of many; and also of the words of our Lord in John: I pray for them; I pray not for the world, but for them whom thou hast given me, because they are thine." [22]

Pope Pius VI condemned the following Jansenist proposition (DZ 1533): "The proposition of the synod (of Pistoia) by which it shows itself eager to remove the cause through which, in part, there has been introduced a forgetfulness of the principles relating to the order of the liturgy, "by recalling it (the liturgy) to a greater simplicity of rites, by expressing it in the vernacular language, by uttering it in a loud voice"; as if the present order of the liturgy, received and approved by the Church, had emanated in some part from the forgetfulness of the principles by which is should be regulated,-rash, offensive to pious ears, insulting to the Church, favorable to the heretics against it."

---

[21] The Catholic Controversy, page 62.
[22] Hebrews 9:28

"As to whether the decree forbidding Catholics to attend the Masses of schismatics and take part in their prayers is to be understood even of the places in which there are no Catholic priests and of prayers in which nothing is contained contrary to Catholic faith and worship", the Council of the Holy Office, August 7, 1704 answered: "His Holiness has decided in the affirmative." (That is, that it is forbidden to take part in the services of schismatics, and therefore those of heretics, since heresy implicitly contains schism.)

The Sacred Congregation for the Propagation of the Faith declared on February 17, 1761: "In no case, even of necessity, is it licit for a Catholic to confess his sins and obtain absolution from a schismatic priest."

Saint Alphonsus (Died 1787) "Hence the devil has always sought to deprive the world of the Mass by means of heretics, constituting them precursors of Antichrist, whose first efforts shall be to abolish the holy sacrifice of the altar, and, according to the prophet Daniel, in punishment of the sins of men, his efforts shall be successful: "And strength was given him against the continual sacrifice because of sins." (Daniel 8:12)" [23]

"It is true that it (the Sacrifice of the Mass) will cease on earth at the time of Antichrist: the Sacrifice of the Mass is to be suspended for twelve hundred and ninety days, that is, for three years and six months and a half, according to the prophesy of Daniel: "And from the time when the continual sacrifice shall be taken away, and the abomination of desolation shall be set up, there shall be a thousand two hundred and ninety days." (Daniel 12:11) [24]

"Hence St. Bonaventure says that in the Mass God manifests to us all the love that He has borne us, and includes in it, as in a compendium, all His benefits. On this account the Devil has always endeavored to abolish the Mass throughout the world by means of heretics, making them the precursors of Antichrist who, before all things, will endeavor to abolish, and in fact will, in punishment for the sins of men, succeed in abolishing the Holy Sacrifice of the Altar,

---

[23] <u>Dignity and Duties of the Priest,</u> pages 211-2
[24] <u>The Blessed Eucharist</u>

according to the prediction of Daniel: "And strength was given him against the continual sacrifice because of sins."" [25]

"In a word, St. John Chrysostom says, that without priests we cannot be saved." [26]

"Without priests, says St. Ignatius Martyr, there would be no saints on this earth." [27]

Dom Gueranger (died 1805) "Further still, she knows that Peter alone can give her the sacred Host. Baptism which makes us to be sons of God, and all the sacraments which multiply the divine energies within us, are a treasure which he alone has license to dispose of legitimately. It is his word, throughout the world, that in every grade of authorized teaching gives birth within souls to faith which is the beginning of salvation, and develops it from these humble commencements right up to the luminous heights of sanctity. Ane because, on the mountain heights, the life of the evangelical counsels is the chosen garden reserved to himself by the Spouse, Peter likewise claims as his own the guidance and protection, in a more special manner, of religious communities; for he wishes to be always able himself to offer directly to Jesus the fairest flowers of that holiness of which his exalted ministry is the very principle and support. Thus sanctified, to Peter again does the Church address herself, when she would learn in what way to approach her Spouse in her worship; she says to him, as heretofore the disciples said to our Lord, "Teach us to pray" (Luke 11:1); and Peter, animated with what he knows so well of the gorgeous pomp of worship in the heavenly country, regulates for us here below the sacred ceremonial, and dictates to the bride herself the theme of her songs. Lastly, who by Peter can add to her holiness those other marks of unity, catholicity, and apostolicity, which are, in the face of the whole world, her unquestionable right and title to govern and to be loved by the Son of God." [28]

---

[25] Saint Alphonsus in The Priest Before the Altar, compiled by F. Macnamara, C.SS.R., 1929, pages 10-11:
[26] Dignity and Duties of the Priest by Saint Alphonsus, referring to Chrysostom's On the Priesthood, 50, 3
[27] Dignity and Duties of the Priest, page 157
[28] The Liturgical Year, Volume XII

Pope Pius IX (died 1878) "He who abandons this See cannot hope to remain within the Church; he who eats the Lamb outside it has no part with God.

The Holy Office on June 22, 1859 declared: "Communication with heretics can be either in a condemned doctrine, or in rites and other signs indicative of adherence to a false sect, with the accompanying scandal of the faithful, to whom the Church therefore forbids this communion, lest the faith be lost or endangered. Whence St. John the Evangelist strictly commands: 'if anyone comes to you and does not bring this (i.e. the Catholic) doctrine, do not receive him into the house, or say to him, Welcome. For he who says to him, Welcome, is sharer in his evil works., II John 20."

Cardinal Manning (died 1892) "Further, he says, "The victim and the sacrifice shall fail, and there shall be in the temple the abomination of desolation." These three passages are taken from the seventh, and the eighth, and the ninth chapters of Daniel. [29]

"3. This leads on plainly to the marks which the prophet gives of the persecution of the last days. Now there are three things which he has recorded. In the foresight of prophecy he saw and noted these three signs The find, that the continual sacrifice shall be taken away; the next, that the sanctuary shall be occupied by the abomination which maketh desolate; the third, that "the strength" and "the stars," as he described it: shall be cast down: and these are the only three I will notice

"Now, first of all what is this "taking away of the continual sacrifice"?

"It was taken away in type at the destruction of Jerusalem. The sacrifice of the Temple, that is, of the lamb, morning and evening, in the Temple of God, was entirely abolished with the destruction of the Temple itself. Now the Prophet Malachias says: "From the rising of the sun even to the going down, any name is great among the Gentiles; and in ovary place there is sacrifice, and there is offered to my name a dean oblation." This passage of the prophet has been interpreted by the Fathers of the Church. beginning with St. Irenaeus, St. Justin Martyr, and I know not how many besides, to be the sacrifice of the Holy

---

[29] Present Crisis of the Holy See, pages 68-9

Eucharist, the true Paschal lamb which came in the place of the type—namely, the sacrifice of Jesus Himself on Calvary renewed perpetually and continued for ever in the sacrifice on the altar. Now has that continual sacrifice been taken away

"That which was typical of it in old days has been already taken away. But has the reality been taken away? The holy Fathers who have written upon the subject of Antichrist, and of these prophecies of Daniel, without a single exception, as far as I know, and they are the Fathers both of the East and of the West, the Greek and the Latin Church—all of them unanimously,—say that in the latter end of the world, during the reign of Antichrist, the holy sacrifice of the altar will cease. In the work on the end of the world, ascribed to St. Hippolytus, after a long description of the afflictions of the last days, we read as follows: "The Churches shall lament with a great lamentation, for there shall be offered no more oblation, nor incense, nor worship acceptable to God. The sacred buildings of the churches shall be as hovels; and the precious body and blood of Christ shall not be manifest in those days; the Liturgy shall be extinct; the chanting of psalms shall cease; the reading of Holy Scripture shall be heard no more. But there shall be upon men darkness, and mourning upon mourning, and woe upon woe." Then, the Church shall be scattered, driven into the wilderness, and shall be for a time, as it was in the beginning, invisible, hidden in catacombs, in dens, in mountains, in lurking-places; for a time it shall be swept, as it were, from the face of the earth- Such is the universal testimony of the Fathers of the early centuries." [30]

As Leo XIII said in the Bull Apostolicae curae: "The Church is forbidden to change, or even touch, the matter or form of any sacrament. She may indeed change or abolish or introduce something in the non-essential rites or 'ceremonial' parts to be used in the administration of the sacraments, such as the processions, prayers or hymns before or after the actual words of the form are recited..."

1917 Code of Canon Law
"It is unlawful for the faithful to assist in any active manner, or to take part in the sacred services of non-Catholics." (Canon 1258)

---

[30] Present Crisis of the Holy See, pages 78-83

"A person who of his own accord and knowingly helps in any manner to propagate heresy, or who communicates in sacred rites (in divinis) with heretics in violation of the prohibition of Canon 1258, incurs suspicion of heresy." (Canon 2316)

Decree: "Wherefore, it is already clear what great care priests ought to take to perform this Sacrament rightly, to see that the matter of both kinds, that is the bread and the wine, be prepared under every safeguard, especially in these times when an insatiable thirst for gain basely tempts many persons to adulterate many substances in such a way that instead of serving for the nourishment of the body they rather do it harm. For many substances are now chemically synthesized, which have the appearance of the genuine article, without the natural substance; and the same result is produced by fraudulently substituting one thing for another in such a way that the fraud is often hard to detect even by chemical analysis." [31]

"Now, in order to be sure of the genuine matter of the bread and wine which is absolutely required in consecrating so great a Sacrament, it will certainly be better, unless the priest have both of these substances made at home, to obtain them from persons who are very expert in them and who actually grind the wheat or press the wine from the grapes: and who, besides, being above all suspicion, can safely certify that they have absolutely without any fraud, made the hosts from wheat alone, and pressed the wine from grapes alone." [32]

Pope Pius XII: "Patriarchs, Archbishops, and other Hierarchs should zealously care for the faithful protection and the accurate observance of their rite, nor are they to permit or to tolerate any change in the rite." [33]

Holy Office warning, 24 July, 1958: "This Supreme Sacred Congregation has learned that in a certain translation of the New Order of Holy Week into the vernacular, the words "mysterium fidei" in the form of the consecration of the chalice are omitted. it is also reported that some priests omit these words in the very celebration of Mass.

---

[31] AAS 21-631, March 26, 1929.

[32] AAS 21-631, March 26, 1929.

[33] Canon 1, paragraph 1 of the Oriental Code of Canon Law. On June 2, 1957 in the fullness of his Apostolic Authority, Pope Pius XII extended this law to the Universal Church

"Therefore this Supreme Congregation gives warning that it is impious to introduce a change in so sacred a matter and to mutilate or alter editions of liturgical books. (See Canon 1399, paragraph 10)

"Bishops therefore, in accordance with the warning of the Holy Office or 14 February, 1958, should see to it that the prescriptions of the sacred canons on divine worship be strictly observed, and they should be closely watchful that no one dare to introduce even the slightest change in the matter and form of the Sacraments."

The Rhine Flows Into the Tiber, page 27: "Cardinal Montini also declared his wholehearted support of the principle that "ceremonies must once again be reduced to a more simple form.""

The Church, by John the Baptist Montini in the early '60's, page 74: "I remember the bleak experience I had in visiting certain cathedrals that were born in the Catholic faith, and remained in that faith for centuries, forming a kind of mystical hearth for the devotion and worship of apostles and fathers, or saints and the christian populace. Later, as these cathedrals were taken over by Protestants, their altars were removed, and I saw as it were a huge decapitated body: the hall was still capable of responding to hymn and prayer, yet something vital seemed to be missing, something like a burnt out fire. And I remember another impression, more tender and no less sorrowful, which I experienced in England this time. I entered magnificent cathedrals and frequently found them empty: for long periods of time empty of the faithful and invariably empty of the heart that for us dwells in the tabernacle-empty, that is, of Christ's mystical and real body. At evening time however the cathedrals became filled with the sweetest of songs, but whence they came I do not know. The whole cathedral seemed to be filled with its own singing, as a single violin producing sweet melodies that at times are as mournful as plaintive wails arising out of statues and tombs, and at other times as serene and brilliant as voices of invisible angels soaring about under those immense gothic vaults."

Vatican II

The Decree on Ecumenism of Vatican II states: "On the other hand, participation in divine worship (communicatio in sacris) may not be considered a means to be used indiscriminately for the restoration of Christian unity. Such participation depends on two basic principles especially: the expression of unity of the Church, and the sharing of the means of grace. The expression of unity very often forbids participation but the grace to be sought sometimes recommends it."

From the Encyclical of Paul VI, Mysterium Fidei, September 3, 1965, the Feast of Saint Pius X "This is why the Fathers felt they had a solemn duty to warn the faithful that, in reflecting upon this most sacred Sacrament, they should not pay attention to the senses, which report only the properties of bread and wine, but rather to the words of Christ, which have power great enough to change, transform, **"transelementize"** the bread and wine into his body and blood."

1967 New All English Canon come sin with for all, although the form is otherwise unchanged.

On April 3, 1969, Montini issued his decree Missale Romanum, which instituted the Novus Ordo Missae, although in many parts of the world it took some time to implement.

"Over the bread: "Take this, all of you, and eat it; this is my Body which will be given up for you." Over the wine: "Take this, all of you, and drink from it; this is the cup of my Blood, the Blood of the new and everlasting covenant. It will be shed for you and for all men so that sins may be forgiven. Do this in memory of me." The words, "The mystery of faith," spoken by the priest are to be taken out of the context of the words spoken by our Lord, and used instead to introduce an acclamation by the faithful." [34]

Notitiae 50, January 1970: "secundum exegetes verbum aramaicum, quod lingua Latina versum est 'pro multis', significationem habet 'pro omnibus': multitude pro qua Christus mortuus est, sine ulla limitatione est, quod idem valet ac dicere: Christus pro omnibus mortuus est. ... According to the exegetes the Aramaic word which in the Latin language is rendered 'pro mutis', has the meaning 'for all': the

---

[34] Caps omitted in the original, from an official translation executed in the early 1970's. Newer translations quote the consecratory form in its original Latin, which retains pro multis, which means for many, instead of for all. However, the official Italian translation from www.Vatican.va retains per tutti, which translates for all, indicating that when the Latin is used, they intend for all, which is the official translation into many languages used universally throughout the world by the Vatican II Church.

multitude whom Christ died for is unlimited, which is the same as saying Christ died for all... "

Notitiae 53, April, 1970: "To the difficulty, which in the words of consecration of the Blood has been excited over interpretations of 'for all men' instead of 'for many', the reply has already been made in Notitiae number 50, January 1970, pages 39-40. Since however some disquiet seems to persist, it seems that the matter should be resumed a little more fully.

"In that reply it is stated: 'according to the exegetes the Aramaic word which in the Latin language is rendered as "for many", has the meaning "for all".

"This statement must be explained with a little more care. Thus as a rule: in the Hebrew (Aramaic) tongue 'all' and 'many' are indicated here by the one designations and there by the other. Therefore strictly speaking the word 'many' does not signify 'all'. But because the word 'many', otherwise that in our western languages, **does not exclude** the totality, it **can** connote this and in fact does mean it, where the context or material subject suggests or demands this. It is not easy to adduce **certain** examples of the phenomenon..." (Emphasis in original)

In March 22, 1973 the Bishop of Superior, Wisconsin issued the following letter: "On May 25, 1972, His Holiness, Pope Paul VI, issued a Pastoral Instruction entitled 'Instruction Concerning Cases When Other Christians May Be Admitted to Eucharistic Communion in the Catholic Church.' A basic reason for the issuing of this Pastoral Instruction is the fact that there have been a number of changed attitudes and practices within the Church of Christ. In various non-Catholic denominations there has been a considerable shift in sacramental theology. ...

"In response to this, Pope Paul's Pastoral Letter gives the following conditions which been to be met for admitting non-Catholic Christians to Holy Communion:

"1. They must believe in the Real Presence of Christ in the Eucharist of the Catholic Church;

"2. They must experience a serious spiritual need; this need is to be understood as a need for an increase in the spiritual life and a need to be incorporated into Christ and united with His members;

"3. They must ask to receive Holy Communion. This means a real desire must be expressed on the part of the non-Catholic Christian."

Declaration of the Sacred Congregation of the Faith, January 25, 1974 AAS 66-661: "The liturgical renewal effected in accord with the Constitution of Vatican Council II, introduced certain changes also in the formulae pertaining to the very essence of the rites of the sacraments. These new words, just like the other words, must be so translated into the vernacular languages that the original meaning be expressed according to the specific character of the languages. Out of this provision have arise some difficulties which are not coming to light when those translations are being sent by the episcopal conferences for the approval of the Apostolic See. In these circumstances, the Sacred Congregation for the Doctrine of the Faith again calls to mind that it is necessary that the translation of the formulae which are essential in the rites of the sacraments should faithfully render the original meaning of the typical, Latin text. In recalling this point, if gives notice:

"After a proposed translation of a sacramental formula into a vernacular language has been duly examined, the Apostolic See, when it believes that the meaning intended by the Church is aptly expressed by the translation, approves and confirms the same, specifying at the same time that the meaning of the translation must be understood according to the mind of the Church as expressed by the original Latin text."

1983 Code of Canon Law

Canon 844/2 of the 1983 Code of Canon Law teaches: "Whenever necessity requires or a genuine spiritual advantage commends it, and provided the danger of error or indifferentism is avoided, Christ's faithful for whom it is physically or morally impossible to approach a catholic minister, may lawfully receive the sacraments of penance, the Eucharist and annointing of the sick from non-catholic ministers in whose Churches these sacraments are valid."

On October 17, 2006, *Cardinal* Arrinze addressed the issue in his official capacity:

"1. A text corresponding to the words *pro multis*, handed down by the Church, constitutes the formula that has been in use in the

Roman Rite in Latin from the earliest centuries. In the past 30 years or so, some approved vernacular texts have carried the interpretive translation "for all", "per tutti", or equivalents.

"2. There is no doubt whatsoever regarding the validity of Masses celebrated with the use of a duly approved formula containing a formula equivalent to "for all", as the Congregation for the Doctrine of the Faith has already declared (cf. Sacra Congregatio pro Doctrina Fidei, *Declaratio de sensu tribuendo adprobationi versionum formularum sacramentalium*, 25 Ianuarii 1974, AAS 66 [1974], 661). Indeed, the formula "for all" would undoubtedly correspond to a correct interpretation of the Lord's intention expressed in the text. It is a dogma of faith that Christ died on the Cross for all men and women (cf. John 11:52; 2 Corinthians 5,14-15; Titus 2,11; 1 John 2,2)."

Last Half of the Twentieth Century

Many prophecies place the Great Apostasy at the end of the twentieth century. In other words, many prophecies have already been fulfilled. We must ask ourselves, why have we missed these things? Has Antichrist come and gone? Did we miss the falling away from the Catholic Faith that is foretold? Something to think about as we study prophecy.

Prophecies

Saint Nilus [35]

"After the year 1900, toward the middle of the 20th century, the people of that time will become unrecognizable. When the time for the advent of the Antichrist approaches, people's minds will grown cloudy from carnal passions, and dishonor and lawlessness will grow stronger. Then the world will become unrecognizable. People's appearances will change, and it will be impossible to distinguish men from women due to their shamelessness in dress and style of hair. These people will be cruel and will be like wild animals because of the temptations of Antichrist. These will be no respect for parents and elders, love will disappear, and Christian pastors, bishops, and priests will become vain men, completely failing to distinguish the righthand way from the left. At that time the morals and traditions of Christians and the Church will change. People will abandon modesty, and dissipation will reign. Falsehood and greed will attain great proportions, and woe to those who pile up treasures. Lust, adultery, homosexuality, secret deeds and murder will rule in society.

"At that future time, due to the power of such great crimes and licentiousness, people will be deprived of the grace of the Holy Ghost, which they received in Holy Baptism, and equally of remorse.

"The Churches of God will be deprived of God-fearing and pious pastors, and woe to Christians remaining in the world at that time; they will completely lose their faith because they will lack the opportunity of seeing the light of knowledge from anyone at all. Then they will

---

[35] Some question the authenticity of this prophecy. It was circulated as a typed page in the very early 1970's and attributed to Saint Nilus. No other information is available on this prophecy. It is included, because of its accuracy.

separate themselves out of the world in holy refuges in search of lightening their spiritual sufferings, but everywhere they will meet obstacles and constraints. And all this will result from the fact that the Antichrist wants to be Lord over everything and become ruler of the whole universe, and he will produce miracles and fantastic signs. He will also give depraved wisdom to an unhappy man so that he will discover a way by which one may can carry on a conversation with another from one end of the earth to the other. At that time men will also fly through the air like birds and descend to the bottom of the sea like fish. And when they have achieved all this, these unhappy people will spend their lives in comfort without knowing, poor souls, that it is deceit of the Antichrist. And the impious one! -- he will so complete science with vanity, that it will go off the right path and lead people to lose faith in the existence of God in these hypostases.

"Then the All-good God will see the downfall of the human race and will shorten the days for the sake of those few who are being saved, because the enemy wants to lead even the chosen into temptation, if that is possible... then the sword of chastisement will suddenly appear and kill the perverter and his servants."

Sister Ludmilla of Prague (cir. 1250)
"Hardly three generations will pass after the world war, when one will also endeavor to prevent the Pope from exercising his sacred office, which will be a sign that the fall of Rome and the end of the world is near."

Jean de Roquetaillade (died 1365)
"Because it is said that twenty centuries after the incarnation of the Word the Beast would also be embodied and she would threaten the earth with evils as impressive as the graces brought by the divine incarnation."

St. Bridget of Sweden (1303-1373)
"Forty years before the year two thousand, the Devil will be let loose for a period to tempt men. When all will seem lost, God Himself will suddenly bring all evil to an end. The sign of when these events will occur will be when priests will have discarded their holy habits and

dress themselves in lay clothes and when women will dress like men and men like women."

Maria Laach Monastery (16th Century)
"The twentieth century will bring death and destruction, apostasy from the Church, discord in families, cities and governments; it will be the century of three great wars with intervals of a few decades. They will become ever more devastating and bloody and will lay in ruins not only Germany, but finally all countries of East and West. After a terrible defeat of Germany will follow the next great war. There will be no bread for people anymore and no fodder for animals. Poisonous clouds, manufactured by human hands, will sink down and exterminate everything. The human mind will be seized by insanity."

Our Lady of Good Fortune Quito Ecuador, February 2, 1634
Mother Mary Anne of Jesus Torres was praying in front of the Blessed Sacrament when suddenly the sanctuary light went out. While she was trying to relight it, a supernatural light filled the church.
"Beloved daughter of My heart, I am Our Lady of Good Fortune, your Mother and Protectress, carrying My Most Holy Son on My left arm and holding the sceptre in My right hand. I have come to tell you some good news: in ten months and ten days you will close your eyes to the earthly light of this world in order to open them to the brightness of light everlasting. Oh, if only human beings and religious knew what Heaven is and what it is to possess God, how differently they would live, sparing no sacrifice in order to enter more fully in possession of it! But some let themselves be dazzled by the false glamour of honours and human greatness while others are blinded by self-love, not realizing that they are falling into lukewarmness, that immense evil which in religious houses destroys their fervor, humility, self-renunciation and the ceaseless practice of religious virtues and fraternal charity, and that child-like simplicity which makes souls so dear to My Divine Son and to Me, their Mother."
Then Our Lady of Good Fortune began to speak of the Order of the Immaculate Conception and in particular of the Convent of the Conception in Quito:
"This house will be attacked with a fury out of hell to destroy and annihilate it, but Divine Providence and I will be watching over to

preserve it, by favouring the virtues practiced by the nuns in this house. ... Know also, My beloved daughter, that My Motherly love will watch over the convents of the Order of My Immaculate Conception, because this Order will give Me great glory through the daughters I shall have here. I shall take special care of the convents formed in this land by the members of this House. Often they will be on the brink of annihilation, but miraculously they will come to life again. Only one will close, in conformity with God's will: you will know which, when you are in Heaven.

"The sanctuary lamp burning in front of the Prisoner of Love, which you saw go out, has many meanings.

"First meaning: at the end of the 19th century and for a large part of the 20th, various heresies will flourish on this earth which will have become a free republic. The precious light of the Faith will go out in souls because of the almost total moral corruption: in those times there will be great physical and moral calamities, in private and in public. The little number of souls keeping the Faith and practicing the virtues will undergo cruel and unspeakable sufferings; through their long drawn out martyrdom many will go to death because of the violence of their sufferings, and those will count as martyrs who gave their lives for Church and for country. To escape being enslaved by these heresies will call for great strength of will, constancy, courage and great trust in God, all of which are gifts from the merciful love of My Divine Son to those He will have chosen for the work of restoration. To put to the trial the faith and trust of these just souls, there will come moments when everything seems lost and paralyzed, and just then comes the happy beginnings of the complete restoration.

"Second meaning: My communities will be abandoned; they will be swamped in a fathomless sea of bitterness, and will seem drowned in tribulations. How many true vocations will be lost for lack of skillful and prudent direction to form them! Each mistress of novices will need to be a soul of prayer, knowing how to discern spirits.

"The third meaning of the lamps going out is that those times the air will be filled with the spirit of impurity which like a deluge of filth will flood the streets, squares and public places. The licentiousness will be such there will be no more virgin souls in the world.

"A fourth meaning is that by having gained control of all the social classes, the sects will tend to penetrate with great skill into the heart of families and destroy even the children. The devil will glory in feeding perfidiously on the heart of children. The innocence of childhood will almost disappear. Thus priestly vocations will be lost, it will be a real disaster. Priests will abandon their sacred duties and will depart from the path marked out for them by God. Then the Church will go through a dark night for lack of a Prelate and Father to watch over it with love, gentleness, strength and prudence and numbers of priest will lost the spirit of God, thus placing their souls in great danger. Pray constantly, cry out unwearingly and weep unceasingly with bitter tears in the depths of your heart, asking Our Father in Heaven, for love of the Eucharistic Heart of My Most Holy Son, for His Precious Blood, so generously shed and for the profound bitterness and sufferings of His Passion and death, that He have pity on His ministers and that He put an end to such fatal times, by sending to His Church the Prelate who will restore the spirit of His priests. Upon this My beloved son, whom My Divine Son and I love with a predilection, we shall heap many gifts, of humility of heart, of docility to varying inspirations, of strength to defend the rights of the Church and of a heart with which he will, like a new Christ, take possession of the mightiest or men as of the lowliest, without scorning the least fortunate among them. With a wholly divine gentleness he will lead consecrated souls to the service of God in religious houses without making the Lord's yoke weigh heavily upon them. He will hold in his hand the scales of the sanctuary for everything to be done in an orderly fashion for God to be glorified. This Prelate and Father will act as a counterweight to the lukewarmness of souls consecrated in the priesthood and in religion. Satan will gain control of this earth through the fault of faithless men who, like a black cloud, will darken the clear sky of the republic consecrated of the Most Sacred Heart of My Divine Son. This republic, having allowed entry to all the vices, will have to undergo all sorts of chastisements, plague, famine, war, apostasy and the loss of souls without number. And to scatter these black clouds blocking the brilliant dawning of the freedom of the Church, there will be a terrible war in which the blood of priests and of religious will flow ... That night will be so horrible that the wickedness will seem triumphant. Then will come My time: in astounding fashion I shall destroy Satan's pride, casting him beneath My feet, chaining him up in the depths of hell, leaving Church and country freed at last from his cruel tyranny.

"The fifth meaning of the lamp's going out is that men possessing great wealth will look on with indifference while the Church is oppressed, virtue is persecuted, and evil triumphs. They will not use their wealth to fight evil and re-construct the Faith. The people will come to care nothing for the things of God, will absorb the spirit of evil and will let themselves be swept away by all vices and passions. Ah, My beloved daughter, were it given you to live in these fatal times, you would die of grief seeing everything I have told you come about. My Most Holy Son and I have such a great love for this earth, our property, that it is our wish as of now to apply your sacrifice and good works to the lessening of the duration of such terrible catastrophes."

Sister Bouquillon (19th century).
"The beginning of the end shall not come in the 19th century, but in the 20th for sure."

Mother Maria Rafols (died 1853)
"He, (the Sacred Heart) , makes me feel that, in the times to come, there shall be in Spain and all over the world, many persecutors of the religion and of the country, who will be anxious to destroy all good things; and my sweet Jesus orders me to write these examples of his protection in order that they may keep up their spirit however big the wars and persecutions might be, having God with them they have nothing to fear. He will confuse the enemies of the Church, and many of them shall become zealous apostles, followers of St. Paul, who will conquer many souls for Him. I do not speak to you for your benefit, but for other sons of Mine, who one day shall be persecuted, and who shall be very uncertain and helpless in the combats prepared by the enemy, who shall try to wipe out not only religion, but even My name from the face of the earth. This period will begin openly in the year 1931.

"I am ready to pour out many graces upon My beloved Spain, which shall be persecuted so severely by Freemasonry. I will not let My faithful sons be overcome. Spain the beloved of My Blessed Mother, is My first beloved, and I would destroy all the nations of the world rather than let the Faith disappear from Spain."

Permanent Instruction of the Alta Vendita (published by order of Pope Pius IX in 1859: "The work which we have undertaken is not the work of a day, nor of a month, nor of a year. It may last many years, a century perhaps, but in our ranks the soldier dies and the fight continues."

An Old German prophecy says: "In the truth you will rejoice, after darkness you will see light, because before the beginning of 2000, the Beast and the Whore will be thrown headlong into the abyss. They will never come forth again. The Sign of the Cross will be resplendent in the glory of light, with faith and law-one flock and one shepherd."

Saint Pius X (died 1914) in E Supremi his first Encyclical: "When all this is considered there is good reason to fear lest this great perversity may be as it were a foretaste, and perhaps the beginning of those evils which are reserved for the last days; and that there may be already in the world the "Son of Perdition" of whom the Apostle speaks (II. *Thess.* ii., 3)."

Archbishop Fulton Sheen

Fulton J. Sheen (1895-1979): "He [Satan] will set up a counterchurch which will be the ape of the Church, because he, the Devil, is the ape of God. It will have all the notes and characteristics of the Church, but in reverse and emptied of its divine content. It will be a mystical body of the Antichrist that will in all externals resemble the mystical body of Christ. [...] But the twentieth century will join the counterchurch because it claims to be infallible when its visible head speaks ex cathedra." [36]

(1950) "We are living in the days of the Apocalypse--the last days of our era.... The two great forces of the Mystical Body of Christ and the Mystical Body of Antichrist are beginning to draw up the battle lines for the catastrophic contest." [37]

---

[36] Communism and the Conscience of the West, Indianapolis: Bobbs-Merrill, 1948, pp. 24-25

[37] Flynn T & L. The Thunder of Justice. Maxkol Communications, Sterling (VA), 1993, p. 20

The Vision of Pope Leo XIII

Exactly 33 years to the day prior to the great Miracle of the Sun in Fatima, that is, on October 13, 1884, Pope Leo XIII had a remarkable vision. When the aged Pontiff had finished celebrating Mass in his private Vatican Chapel, attended by a few Cardinals and members of the Vatican staff, he suddenly stopped at the foot of the altar. He stood there for about 10 minutes, as if in a trance, his face ashen white. Then, going immediately from the Chapel to his office, he composed the above prayer to St. Michael, with instructions it be said after all Low Masses everywhere.

When asked what had happened, he explained that, as he was about to leave the foot of the altar, he suddenly heard voices - two voices, one kind and gentle, the other guttural and harsh. They seemed to come from near the tabernacle. As he listened, he heard the following conversation:

The guttural voice, the voice of Satan in his pride, boasted to Our Lord: "I can destroy your Church."

The gentle voice of Our Lord: "You can? Then go ahead and do so."

Satan: "To do so, I need more time and more power."

Our Lord: "How much time? How much power?

Satan: "75 to 100 years, and a greater power over those who will give themselves over to my service."

Our Lord: "You have the time, you will have the power. Do with them what you will."

The Third Secret of Fatima

The Third Secret has two parts. One part is the logical continuation of the words: "In Portugal, the dogma of the Faith will be always preserved, etc." The other concerns the Pope.

It was placed in two envelopes with instructions to the Bishop of Fatima and to the Cardinal Patriarch of Lisbon to open and reveal it in 1960. Sister Lucy said it would be more clear in 1960. Note well that the Pope is not asked to reveal it at this time, probably because the Blessed Virgin Mary knew there would be no Pope and mentioned this in the Secret.

We have some clues, including several statements of which from Jacinta: "I don't know how it was, but I saw the Holy Father in a very big house, kneeling before a table with his hands before his face, crying. He went to the door of the house and there were lots of people there throwing stones and cursing and saying horrible words. Poor Holy Father! We must pray for him too." It is said that Jacinta made one statement concerning the Pope and Lucia told her to back off, it is close to the secret. "Lucy, Lucy, can't you see all the people, on the roads and in the fields, crying and dying of hunger, with not a things to eat? And the Holy Father praying to the Immaculate Heart of Mary and all the people praying with him?"

"One day, two priests recommended us to pray for the Holy Father, and explained to us who the Pope was. Afterwards, Jacinta asked me: "Is he the one I saw weeping, the one Our Lady told us about in the Secret?" "Yes, he is."

In early 1959 Sister Lucy asked to go on the radio and talk to the world about Fatima. Did she already see the third secret being fulfilled? On July 2, 1959 *Sr. Lucy* replied to a request from the Church for comments on an interview she had given father Fuentes two years earlier. This interview was quite apocalyptic. She denied everything that Father Fuentes had reported. However, there is strong evidence that this *Sr. Lucy* was not Lucia dos Santos, but an imposter.

Interview with Sister Lucy

On December 26, 1957 Father Augustin Fuentes, who was preparing to become the postulator of the causes for beatification of Francisco and Jacinta Marto, met with Sister Lucy at her convent in Coimbra, Portugal. Here, he was able to converse with the Fatima seer at great length. Upon his return to his native Mexico, he gave a conference on the meeting, in which he reported Sister Lucy's words. Father Alonso, the official Fatima archivist for 16 years, stressed that the account of this conference was published "with every guarantee of authenticity and with due episcopal approval, including that of the Bishop of Fatima."

Father Fuentes affirmed that the message came "from the very lips of the principal seer."

Sources: This matter has been documented at length by Frère Michel de la Sainte Trinité in Volume III of his series The Whole Truth About Fatima. The following text is The Fatima Crusader's translation of the Spanish and the English texts published in Frère Michel's book The Third Secret (Volume III, pp. 336-338). The subtitles have been added for your convenience.

The Report by Father Fuentes

"I wish to tell you about the last conversation which I had with Sister Lucy on the 26th of December (last year). I met her in her convent. She was very sad, very pale and emaciated. She said to me,"

"Father, the most Holy Virgin is very sad because no one has paid any attention to Her Message, neither the good nor the bad. The good continue on their way, but without giving any importance to Her Message. The bad, not seeing the punishment of God actually falling upon them, continue their life of sin without even caring about the Message. But believe me, Father, God will chastise the world and this will be in a terrible manner. The punishment from Heaven is imminent."

"Father, how much time is there before 1960 arrives? It will be very sad for everyone, not one person will rejoice at all if beforehand the world does not pray and do penance. I am not able to give any other details, because it is still a Secret. According to the will of the Most Holy Virgin, only the Holy Father and the Bishop of Fatima are permitted to know the Secret, but they have chosen to not know it so that they would not be influenced. This is the third part of the Message of Our Lady, which will remain secret until 1960."

"Tell them, Father, that many times the Most Holy Virgin told my cousins Francisco and Jacinta, as well as myself, that many nations will disappear from the face of the earth. She said that Russia will be the instrument of chastisement chosen by Heaven to punish the whole world if we do not beforehand obtain the conversion of that poor nation."

Sister Lucy also told me: "Father, the devil is in the mood for engaging in a decisive battle against the Blessed Virgin. And the devil knows what it is that offends God the most, and which in a short space of time will gain for him the greatest number of souls. Thus the devil does everything to overcome souls consecrated to God, because in this way the devil will succeed in leaving the souls of the faithful abandoned by their leaders, thereby the more easily will he seize them."

"That which afflicts the Immaculate Heart of Mary and the Heart of Jesus is the fall of religious and priestly souls. The devil knows that religious and priests who fall away from their beautiful vocation drag numerous souls to hell. ... The devil wishes to take possession of consecrated souls. He tries to corrupt them in order to lull to sleep the souls of laypeople and thereby lead them to final impenitence. He employs all tricks, even going so far as to suggest the delay of entrance into religious life. Resulting from this is the sterility of the interior life, and among the laypeople, coldness (lack of enthusiasm) regarding the subject of renouncing pleasures and the total dedication of themselves to God."

"Tell them also, Father, that my cousins Francisco and Jacinta sacrificed themselves because in all the apparitions of the Most Holy Virgin, they always saw Her very sad. She never smiled at us. This sadness, this anguish which we noted in Her, penetrated our souls. This sadness is caused by the offenses against God and the punishments which menace sinners. And so, we children did not know what to think except to invent various means of praying and making sacrifices."

The other things which sanctified these children was to see the vision of Hell.

"Father, that is why my mission is not to indicate to the world the material punishments which are certain to come if the world does not pray and do penance beforehand. No! My mission is to indicate to everyone the imminent danger we are in of losing our souls for all eternity if we remain obstinate in sin."

Sister Lucy also said to me: "Father, we should not wait for an appeal to the world to come from Rome on the part of the Holy Father, to do penance. Nor should we wait for the call to penance to come from our bishops in our diocese, nor from the religious congregations. No! Our Lord has already very often used these means, and the world has not paid attention. That is why now, it is necessary for each one of us to begin to reform himself spiritually. Each person must not only save his own soul but also help to save all the souls that God has placed on our path."

"The devil does all in his power to distract us and to take away from us the love for prayer; we shall be saved together or we shall be damned together."

"Father, the Most Holy Virgin did not tell me that we are in the last times of the world, but She made me understand this for three reasons."

"The first reason is because She told me that the devil is in the mood for engaging in a decisive battle against the Virgin. And a decisive battle is the final battle where one side will be victorious and the other side will suffer defeat. Also, from now on we must choose sides. Either we are for God or we are for the devil. There is no other possibility."

"The second reason is because She said to my cousins as well as to myself, that God is giving two last remedies to the world. These are the Holy Rosary and devotion to the Immaculate Heart of Mary. These are the last two remedies which signify that there will be no others."

"The third reason is because in the plans of Divine Providence, God always, before He is about to chastise the world, exhausts all other remedies. Now, when He sees that the world pays no attention whatsoever, then as we say in our imperfect manner of speaking, He offers us with 'certain fear' the last means of salvation, His Most Holy Mother. It is with 'certain fear' because if you despise and repulse this ultimate means, we will not have any more forgiveness from Heaven, because we will have committed a sin which the Gospel calls the sin against the Holy Ghost. This sin consists of openly rejecting, with full knowledge and consent, the salvation which He offers. Let us remember that Jesus Christ is a very good Son and that He does not permit that we offend and despise His Most Holy Mother. We have recorded through many centuries of Church history the obvious testimony which demonstrates by the terrible chastisements which have befallen those who have attacked the honor of His Most Holy Mother, how Our Lord Jesus Christ has always defended the honor of His Mother."

Sister Lucy told me: "The two means for saving the world are prayer and sacrifice."

Regarding the Holy Rosary, Sister Lucy said: "Look, Father, the Most Holy Virgin, in these last times in which we live, has given a new efficacy to the recitation of the Rosary. She has given this efficacy to such an extent that there is no problem, no matter how difficult it is, whether temporal or above all spiritual, in the personal life of each one of us, of our families, of the families of the world or of the religious communities, or even of the life of peoples and nations, that cannot be solved by the Rosary. There is no problem I tell you, no matter how difficult it is, that we cannot resolve by the prayer of the Holy Rosary. With the Holy Rosary we will save ourselves. We will sanctify ourselves. We will console Our Lord and obtain the salvation of many souls."

"Finally, devotion to the Immaculate Heart of Mary, our Most Holy Mother, consists in considering Her as the seat of mercy, of goodness and of pardon, and as the sure door by which we are to enter Heaven."

Evils of the Time

Prophecies

II Timothy 3:1-9

"Know also this, that, in the last days, shall come dangerous times. Men shall be lovers of themselves, covetous, haughty, proud, blasphemers, disobedient to parents, ungrateful, wicked, Without affection, without peace, slanderers, incontinent, unmerciful, without kindness, Traitors, stubborn, puffed up, and lovers of pleasures more than of God: Having an appearance indeed of godliness, but denying the power thereof. Now these avoid. For of these sort are they who creep into houses, and lead captive silly women laden with sins, who are led away with divers desires: Ever learning, and never attaining to the knowledge of the truth. Now as Jannes and Mambres resisted Moses, so these also resist the truth, men corrupted in mind, reprobate concerning the faith. But they shall proceed no farther; for their folly shall be manifest to all men, as theirs also was."

II Timothy 4:3-4

"For there shall be a time, when they will not endure sound doctrine; but, according to their own desires, they will heap to themselves teachers, having itching ears: And will indeed turn away their hearing from the truth, but will be turned unto fables."

II Peter 3:3-5

"Knowing this first, that in the last days there shall come deceitful scoffers, walking after their own lusts, Saying: Where is his promise or his coming? for since the time that the fathers slept, all things continue as they were from the beginning of the creation. For this they are wilfully ignorant of, that the heavens were before, and the earth out of water, and through water, consisting by the word of God."

St. Anthony of the Desert (4th Century) [Disquisition CXIV].

"Men will surrender to the spirit of the age. They will say that if they had lived in our day, Faith would be simple and easy. But in their day, they will say, things are complex; the Church must be brought up to date and made meaningful to the day's problems. When the Church and the World are one, then those days are at hand. Because our Divine Master placed a barrier between His things and the things of the world.

"And after these shall arise Antichrist and having by the signs and lying wonders of his magical deceit, beguiled the Jews as though he were the expected Christ, he shall afterwards characterize himself by all kinds of excesses of cruelty and lawlessness...and he shall perpetrate such things for 3 years and 6 months.

"Antichrist will exceed in malice, perversity, lust, wickedness, impiety, and ruthlessness and barbarity all men that have ever disgraced human nature. Hence St. Paul emphatically calls him 'the man of sin, the son of perdition, the wicked one, whose birth and coming is through the operation of Satan, in all manner of seduction and iniquity.' (2 Thess., 2). Through his great power, deceit and malice he shall succeed in decoying or forcing to his worship two thirds of mankind; the remaining third part of men will continue true to the faith and worship of Jesus Christ most steadfastly. But in his satanic rage and fury, Antichrist will persecute these brave and devout Christians during three years and a half, and torture them with such an extremity of barbarity, with all the old and newly invented instruments of pain, as to exceed all past persecutors of the Church combined. He will oblige all his followers to bear impressed upon their foreheads or right hands the mark of the Beast and will starve to death all those who refuse to receive it."

St Vincent Ferrer (1350-1419):

"Be warned that there will come a time of religious laxity and of catastrophes such as will never have been seen or be seen again. In that time, women will dress like men and will behave as they like and in a licentious manner; and men will demean themselves by dressing like women. But God shall purify and regenerate all things and sadness shall be converted to joy."

The Persecution of Antichrist

One of the evils of this time is the persecution of Antichrist, upon which some little is said.

Saint John Eudes says: "Pray especially for those who will have to suffer the persecution of antichrist at the end of the world, for it will be the most cruel and horrible of all persecutions."

The Devil, Father Delacourte: ""Our final end", wrote one of the high dignitaries of that gloomy empire, in 1819, "our final end is that of Voltaire and the French revolution, the annihilation of Catholicity, and even of the Christian idea forever." This, then, is their (the secret societies) object. Another will give a sketch of the proceedings: "It is decided in our councils that we want no more Christians. Let us make no martyrs, but make vice popular among the masses. Let them breathe it through the fives senses. Make hearts vicious, and you will have no more Catholics!" If that be not diabolical language, what is?"

The Devil, Father Delacourte: "This mystery of iniquity is partially accomplished; the Catholic Church is not crumbling away, and will not crumble away; but the infernal church is being formed and disciplined. It has hatred for its bond. It gives the first place to those who must hate Jesus Christ and His mystical body; it swells its ranks from the indifferent themselves, because he who is not for Jesus Christ is against Him. Men who would neither kill, nor rob, alas! Men who go to Mass, and who, in spite of the repeated **anathema** of the Holy See, approach the Holy Table, will declare to us upon their honor that they belong to a secret society, Freemasonry, for instance, and that there all religious opinions are respected, not excepting their own."

Dom Gueranger commenting on Saints John and Paul (June 27, martyrs in latter part of the fourth century): "Merely to preclude Christians from public offices, and to prohibit them from holding chairs for the teaching of youth, that was all the apostate aimed at! However, the blood which he wanted to avoid shedding must flow, even though a hypocrites hands be dyed therewith; for, according to the divine plan, bloodshed alone can bring extreme situations to an issue, and never was holy Church menaced with greater peril." (This was the time of Julian the Apostate). "... Verily, by the martyrdom of the faithful does Christ triumph. ... Woe to the day wherein the deceptive mirage of guileful peace mislead minds; wherein, merely because sin does not stare them in the face, Christian souls stoop from the lofty standpoint of their Baptism, to compromises which even a pagan world would avoid. Glorious brethren! Make the children of holy Church turn aside from the fatal error, which would lead them to misconceptions of sacred traditions received by them in heritage. Maintain the sons of God at the full height of noble sentiments demanded by their heavenly origin, by the throne that awaits them, by the divine Blood they daily drink; far from them be all such base notions as would be calculated to excite against their heavenly Father the blasphemies of the accursed city! Nowadays has arisen a persecution not dissimilar to that in which you gained the crown; Julian's plan of action is once more in vogue; if these mimics of the apostate do not equal him in intelligence, that at least surpass him in hatred and hypocrisy. But God is no more wanting to His church now than he as then; obtain for us the grace to do our part in the resistance, as was done by you, and the victory will be the same."

Infiltration of the Catholic Church

The enemies of the Catholic Church in order to fulfill Voltaire's idea have declared they wish to infiltrate the Church.

"That We should act without delay in this matter is made imperative especially by the fact that the <u>partisans of error are to be sought not only among the Church's open enemies; but, what is to be most dreaded and deplored, in her very bosom, and are the more mischievous the less they keep in the open.</u> We allude, Venerable Brethren, to many who belong to the Catholic laity, and, what is much more sad, to the ranks of the priesthood itself, who, animated by a false zeal for the Church, lacking the solid safeguards of philosophy and theology, nay more, thoroughly imbued with the poisonous doctrines taught by the enemies of the Church, and lost to all sense of modesty, put themselves forward as reformers of the Church; and, forming more boldly into line of attack, assail all that is most sacred in the work of Christ, not sparing even the Person of the Divine Redeemer, whom, with sacrilegious audacity, they degrade to the condition of a simple and ordinary man.", Pope Saint Pius X, in the Encyclical <u>Pascendi Dominici Gregis</u>, September 8, 1907.

Excerpts From the <u>Permanent Instruction of the Alta Vendita</u>

This was provided to Pope Pius IX, who ordered it published in 1859: [38]

"The work which we have undertaken is not the work of a day, nor of a month, nor of a year. It may last many years, a century perhaps, but in our ranks the soldier dies and the fight continues.

"We do not mean to win the Popes to our cause, to make them neophytes of our principles, and propagators of our ideas. That would be a ridiculous dream, no matter in what manner events may turn. Should cardinals or prelates, for example, enter, willingly or by surprise, in some manner, into a part of our secrets, it would be by no means a motive to desire their elevation to the See of Peter. That elevation would destroy us. Ambition alone would bring them to apostasy from us. The needs of power would force them to immolate us. That which we ought to demand, that which we should seek and expect, as the Jews expected the Messiah, is a Pope according to our wants."

"Now then, in order to secure to us a Pope in the manner required, it is necessary to fashion for that Pope a generation worthy of the reign of which we dream. Leave on one side old age and middle life, go to the youth, and, if possible, even to infancy. Never speak in their presence a word of impiety or impurity, Maxima debetur puero reverentia. Never forget these words of the poet for they will preserve you from licences which it is absolutely essential to guard against for the good of the cause. In order to reap profit at the home of each family, in order to give yourself the right of asylum at the domestic hearth, you ought to present yourself with all the appearance of a man grave and moral. Once your reputation is established in the colleges, in the gymnasiums, in the universities, and in the seminaries-once that you shall have captivated the confidence of professors and students, so act that those who are principally engaged in the ecclesiastical state should love to seek your conversation. Nourish their souls with the splendours of ancient Papal Rome. There is always at the bottom of the Italian heart a regret for Republican Rome. Excite, enkindle those natures so full of warmth and of patriotic fire. Offer them at first, but

---

[38]   The complete instruction may be obtained in <u>Key Documents to Understanding the Great Apostasy</u>.

always in secret, inoffensive books, poetry resplendent with national emphasis; then little by little you will bring your disciples to the degree of cooking desired. When upon all the points of the ecclesiastical state at once, this daily work shall have spread our ideas as the light, then you will be able to appreciate the wisdom of the counsel in which we take the initiative."

"That reputation will open the way for our doctrines to pass to the bosoms of the young clergy, and go even to the depths of convents. In a few years the young clergy will have, by the force of events, invaded all the functions. They will govern, administer, and judge. They will form the council of the Sovereign. They will be called upon to choose the Pontiff who will reign; and that Pontiff, like the greater part of his contemporaries, will be necessarily imbued with the Italian and humanitarian principles which we are about to put in circulation. It is a little grain of mustard which we place in the earth, but the sun of justice will develop it even to be a great power; and you will see one day what a rich harvest that little seed will produce."

Excerpts from AA-1025

A piece was distributed called The Story of Seminary Student 1025, which has been fictionalized as AA-1025. These excerpts are from this true story of a Communist infiltrator into the seminaries, who infiltrated in 1937: [39]

"The six years of study completed, Mikolaj, now 20, was called to the office of the Uncle who told him point-blank: "I am going to send you abroad to become a militant atheist on the world scene. Your main duty will be to fight all religions, but the Catholic religion in particular because of its efficient structures. In order to achieve this you will enter a seminary and become a Catholic priest. But you must return to Poland and seek reconciliation with your foster parents who will be delighted to hear of your "vocation" and who will help you to become a priest."

The Uncle gave him further instructions and reminders: "Persecution is useless; we don't want any martyrs as long as we are not in complete control of the West. Religion must be destroyed by

---

[39]   The complete instruction may be obtained in Key Documents to Understanding the Great Apostasy.

dialectics. [Dialectic: The art or practice of examining statements logically as by question and answer.] You are to send me a report every week. After a while you will be put in touch with the rest of the network and you will be responsible for ten other agents; but you will not know who they are, and they will not know you. To reach them and to reach you everything will go through this office. We already have many priests in those countries which are afflicted with Catholicism, one is a bishop. ... You will receive letters from us. You will recognize every letter as genuine by the code numbers SS 1025, which is your own. SS means Seminary Student. Yes, there are 1024 others."

"Mikolaj went on: "We must put it into their heads, and especially priests, that the time has come to seek and work for the merging of all religions. We must, in particular, promote among Catholics a feeling of guilt concerning the "ONE TRUTH" which they claim they alone possess. We must convince them that this attitude is a monstrous sin of pride, and that they must now seek reconciliation with other religions. This thought must be made to grow and be uppermost in their minds."

"Answered the Uncle: "Very well! But don't you think that this scheme is somewhat unrealistic?" - "Not at all!", said "Mikolaj, "I myself was a Catholic up to the age of 15, and a very devout one at that; I think it should be comparatively easy to convince Catholics that there are holy persons among Protestants, Mussulmans [Muslims] and Jews. And since they are holy, they also are the members of the "Communion of Saints" in which Catholics believe. Starting from this, we will say that to keep these people out of the Church is an insult to God. Of course, we shall drop the term "Communion of Saints"; we shall substitute for it some other expression such as "Community of Believers" or "People of God"."

""The merging of all religions", continues Mikolaj in his confessions, "and the brotherhood of man, must always be re-asserted as the basic motivation for all the changes. "Love thy neighbor as thyself" will be our scriptural justification. The greatest change, and the most desirable one, is the suppression of the papacy; but this appeared very difficult to me in view of Christ's promise: "Thou art the Rock, and upon this Rock I shall build my Church". We shall therefore endeavour to undermine the authority of the pope in every possible way, and we shall try to enlist his (the pope's) cooperation to introduce the changes that will make this possible. We shall promote the concept of Episcopal Equality and the priesthood of the laity."'"

"'"In the Mass, the words "Real Presence" and "Transubstantiation" must be deleted. We shall speak of "Meal" and "Eucharist" instead. We shall destroy the Offertory and play down the Consecration and, at the same time, we shall stress the part played by the people. In the Mass, as it is today, the priest turns his back to the people and fills a sacrificial function which is intolerable. He appears to offer his Mass to the great Crucifix hanging over the ornate altar. We shall pull down the Crucifix, substitute a table for the altar, and turn it around so that the priest may assume a presidential function. The priest will speak to the people much more than before: to achieve this, we shall shorten what is now called the Mass proper, and we shall add many readings to what is called the Foremass. In this manner the Mass will gradually cease to be regarded as an act of adoration to God, and will become a gathering and an act of human brotherhood. All these points will have to be elaborated in great detail and they may take anything up to 30 years before they are implemented, but I think that all my objectives will be fulfilled by 1974."'"

Saint John Eudes on the Universal Conversion

These same words are also understood to mean all the poor whose hearts are detached from the things of earth, who love and embrace poverty for the love of Him Who, possessing all the treasure of divinity, willed to become poor for love of us that we might possess eternal riches. But we must understand the text to refer particularly to those who have voluntarily stripped themselves of all things through the holy vow of poverty, in order to imitate our divine Saviour and His most holy Mother more perfectly in their state of poverty, which was so extreme that the Son of God uttered these words: "The foxes have holes, and the birds of the air nests: but the son of man hath not where to lay His head." [40] Oh, what great treasures are encompassed by this voluntary poverty, since our Lord Himself said: "Blessed are ye poor, for yours is the Kingdom of God." [41] Oh, how dangerous is the possession of worldly wealth, since He Who is eternal truth also said: "Woe to you that are rich, for you have your consolation!" [42] And speaking through St. Paul, He utters these terrible words: "They that will become rich, fall into temptation, and into the snare of the devil, and into many unprofitable and hurtful desires, which drown men into destruction and perdition." [43] That is why, if you love riches, do not love the false riches of this world but the true wealth of heaven, which is the fear and love of God, charity toward your neighbor, humility, obedience, patience, purity, and the other Christian virtues which will lead you to the possession of an eternal empire.

This explanation of the aforementioned word, *esurientes*, (humble), is highly comforting. It is also a prophecy of the most holy Mother of God, referring to the enormous task yet to be accomplishes of converting the infidels, Jews, heretics and false Christians throughout the world. [44] It was foretold and proclaimed long ago by the oracle of Holy Scripture, by the mouth of the Church, and by the voices of the Fathers, Doctors and saints through the Spirit of God has spoken.

---

[40] Matthew 8:20

[41] Luke 6:20

[42] Luke 6:24

[43] I Timothy 6:9

[44] Notice the distinction between heretics and false Christians. Heretics are outside of the Church, even if they are in good Faith as some Protestants are. However, false Christians are in the Church, but not living the Catholic way of life.

Open the sacred books and there you will hear the divine Spirit speaking of our Lord through the mouth of the royal prophet, assuring us that Christ will rule and reign throughout the world, [45] that all the kinds of the earth will adore Him and all peoples will serve Him; [46] that all tribes will be blessed in Him and all nations will magnify Him; [47] that the whole universe will be filled with His glory; [48] that all generations without exception will adore Him and glorify His holy name; [49] that the whole world will be converted to Him; and that all the tribes of the world will fall prostrate before His face to adore Him. [50]

Do you not hear the eternal Father, speaking to His Divine Son in the second Psalm, promise Him, as His inheritance, all the nations of the world and possession of the entire earth? [51]

Do you not hear the Church so often praying thus to God: "Let all the earth adore Thee and sing to Thee: let it sing a psalm to Thy Name?" [52] Are you not familiar with the solemn prayers offered by Holy Church each year on Good Friday for the sanctification of all her children and the conversion of all heretics, Jews and pagans? Do you now know that every day she obliges her priests to offer the Holy Sacrifice of the Mass to God for all men and to implore the salvation of the world in these words: "We offer unto Thee, O Lord, the chalice of salvation, beseeching Thy clemency, that it may rise up in the sight of Thy divine majesty, as a savor of sweetness, for our salvation, and for that of the whole world?" Tell me then, I beg of you, would the Holy Ghost Who animates and guides the Church in all things permit her to offer prayers that were futile and unheard?

This great general conversion has been revealed by the Spirit of God not only to the prophets of the Old Law but also to the holiest men and women of the New Law. Does not the great Apostle St. Paul ensure us that all the Jews will be converted, and that their conversion will be followed by that of the whole world? There is every reason to believe that God will not refuse His Grace to all other men.

---

[45] Psalm 71:8
[46] Psalm 71:11
[47] Psalm 71:17
[48] Psalm 71:19
[49] Psalm 85:9
[50] Psalm 21:29
[51] Psalm 2:8
[52] Psalm 65:4

Our Lord said one day to St. Brigid, whose revelations have been approved by three Popes and two General Councils: "The time will come when there will be but one fold, one shepherd and one faith, and when God will be known to all." [53]

"You must realize," Christ revealed to her on another occasion, "that pagans will have such great devotion that Christian will be only their servants in the spiritual life, and then shall we seethe fulfillment of the Scriptures, which say that the people who know Me not will glorify Me, and that the deserts will be edified. At that time all will sing: Glory be to the Father, to the Son and to the Holy Ghost, and honor to all the saints!" [54]

All the holy Fathers [55] agree that after the death of antichrist the whole world will be converted, and although some of them assert that the world will last but a few days after his death, while others say a few months, some authorities insist that it will continue to exist many years after. St. Catherine of Sienna, St. Vincent Ferrer, St. Francis of Paula and a number of other saints have predicted this ultimate universal conversion.

Then shall we witness the fulfillment of this great prophecy of the Queen of prophets: *Esurientes implevit bonis*, although not perhaps so perfectly as we might wish; that is, with no one left on earth who did not know and love God. But if this conversion is not completely general, it will prove, nonetheless, a delicious and magnificent feast for all those who possess a great hunger and burning thirst for he glory of God and the salvation of souls. They will be overwhelmed with inconceivable happiness and joy upon seeing their Creator and Saviour known, served and honored throughout the world, together with His most worthy Mother, and beholding demons who now possess so many rich treasures on earth-that is, so many souls of infidels, heretics and bad Catholics-dispossessed of all, according to these divine words: "And the rich He hath sent away empty."

Even if this prophecy is not completely fulfilled here on earth, it will find its entire and perfect fulfillment in heaven, where the insatiable hunger and burning thirst possessed by all the saints during their earthly lives for the glory of God and the salvation of souls will be

---

[53] Revelations Book six Chapter 77
[54] Revelations Book 6 Chapter 83
[55] Dionysius the Carthusian in cap. 3, Epist. 1, ad Thess; Cornelius a Lapide in cap. 2, Epist. Ad Rom. Verse 15.

perfectly satiated and slaked, and these words will be fulfilled in each of them: "I shall be satisfied when Thy glory shall appear." [56] There is no mind capable of understanding, nor tongue of expressing, the least particle of the inestimable and inexpressible blessing which God will shower upon them for their great zeal in promoting His honor on earth, and for the salvation of the souls whom they have delivered from the possession of the devil.

O Mother of Mercy, who by thy prayers and merits didst hasten the time of the Incarnation of the Saviour of the world, hasten too, we pray thee, the desireable time of this great conversion which is so necessary for the salvation of so many souls who perish daily. Alas, take pity on them, O Mother of grace, and pray to thy Son to have pity on all the works of His hands, to have compassion on them because of the many sufferings which His holy humanity endured and the Precious Blood that He shed in order to save these souls from falling into hell.

---

[56] Psalm 16:13

Has Antichrist Come and Gone Unnoticed?

Much could be written on Antichrist and there is much speculation. First of all we must remember what Jesus warned us of these times: "For there shall arise false Christs and false prophets, and shall shew great signs and wonders, insomuch as to deceive (if possible) even the elect." [57] Yes, the elect can and were deceived by Antichrist.

Note well that we are certain on a few things. One of these is that Antichrist will take away the Holy Sacrifice of the Mass as we saw above. And so we must ask ourselves, has the Mass been taken away? The answer is yes it has been taken away by Paul VI. When he replaced it with the Novus Ordo Missae.

In the Novus Ordo Missae instead of offering up the spotless host and the chalice of salvation, the fruit of the earth and work of human hands as well as the fruit of the vine and the work of human hands.

The key thing to note is that for decades most vernacular translations used the words *for all* instead of the words *for many* in the consecration of the wine. This would invalidate the consecration of the wine for it is a substantial change in the essential words of the Mass, as Paul VI declared: "The liturgical renewal effected in accord with the Constitution of Vatican Council II, introduced certain changes also in the formulae pertaining to the very essence of the rites of the sacraments."

Some might object that these words are not necessary for a valid consecration. Others might object that the Latin retained the words *pro multis*, which translates as *for many*. However, these words must be understood in the light of the two *notitiae*, which gives these words the meaning *for all*. In fact, this might even effect the intention of a priest using the *extraordinary form* or *John XXIII Mass*.

Father Carl Pulvermacher said in 1976: "When they have gotten rid of all of the priests with the New Rite of Ordination, then they will give us the Mass back." He was right. The New Rite of Ordination has had *changes also in the formulae pertaining to the very essence of the rites of the sacrament.*

Old Form of the consecration of a Bishop: "Fill up in Thy priest the perfection of Thy ministry, and sanctify him with the dew of Thy

---

[57] Matthew 24:24

heavenly ornaments of all beauty." New Form: "So now pour out upon this chosen one that power which is from you the governing spirit when you gave to your beloved Son, Jesus Christ, the Spirit given by him to the holy apostles, who founded the Church in every place to be your temple for the unceasing glory and praise of your name."

Old Form of the ordination of a priest: "Give we beseech thee, Almighty Father, the dignity of priesthood on these thy servants; renew in their hearts the spirit of sanctity, so that they may hold this office of the second order (second rank), which they have received from Thee and by the example of their life impart a worthy criterion of conduct." New Form: "Almighty Father, grant to these of yours the dignity of the priesthood. Renew within them the Spirit of holiness. As CO-WORKERS with the order of bishops, may they be faithful to the ministry that they receive from you, Lord God, and be to others a model of right conduct."

E Sylvester Berry comments: "This indicates that Antichrist and his prophet will introduce ceremonies to imitate the Sacraments of the Church." [58] Paul VI did just this changing the rites of all of the Sacraments, except the essential Rite of Baptism, which is Scriptural. In reading the Biblical Marks of Antichrist one soon sees that he fulfills them all. He changed times and laws by instituting a new calendar with his *New Mass*. He was destroyed by the *brightness of Jesus' coming* by dying on the Feast of the Transfiguration.

And so we are *after* the death of Antichrist, awaiting the Three Days of Darkness and the Conversion of the world as foretold by the prophets and others. It is recommended to read <u>Key Documents to Understanding the Great Apostasy</u> and <u>54 Years that Changed the Catholic Church</u>. Also reread the sections on Antichrist and the Mass above in light of this new information.

Brother Hermenegild TOSF

---

[58] <u>The Apocalypse of Saint John</u>, page 138 commenting on Apocalypse 13:16

Made in United States
North Haven, CT
23 April 2025